A Peaceful Mind

❖

Bernie Kirwan

ORIGINAL WRITING

© 2008 Bernie Kirwan

Front cover photography (Chestnut Walk, Courtown Woods, County Wexford) and back cover author portrait by Kay MacDonald.

ISBN: 978-1-906018-38-2

A CIP catalogue for this book is available from the National Library.

Printed in Ireland
Published by Original Writing Ltd., Dublin, 2008

To Michael, Eoin, Niall, and Mary

CONTENTS

Foreword

WE ARE PRIVILEGED IN IRELAND in 2008 to live in a time of opportunity and plenty. The pace of life has however increased hugely, to the extent that it is often easy to be swept along by the tide of commercialism and to lose sight of the important things in life. Good health is something we often take for granted and it is therefore all the more shocking when a serious illness develops.

As a Medical Oncologist, I witness every day the impact that a diagnosis of cancer has—not alone on the person diagnosed with this feared illness but on his or her entire family. Often this the person's first encounter with ill-health. Plucked from the healthy 'Outside World', they are suddenly faced with a potentially life-threatening illness and the fear of an uncertain future can seem absolutely overpowering. The urgency of the situation often means that treatments need to be undertaken quickly—surgery, chemotherapy, radiotherapy—again often the first exposure in a person's life to these treatments, adding additional trauma to the whole experience. The journey from diagnosis, through treatment and to cancer survivorship is unique for each individual and its course is no doubt, at least in part, shaped by a persons previous life experience, personality, coping skills, family and social support.

Acceptance of the new life circumstances does not happen overnight and is a gradual process. Like every difficult life event, facing a cancer diagnosis is easier if you are fore-warned and forearmed. I believe *A Peaceful Mind* goes a long way towards achieving both of those goals. There is no substitute for learning from someone who has experienced something first hand.

Bernie Kirwan is a very clear thinking, courageous young woman who has been through a serious cancer illness and emerged out the other side by her own admission—stronger, with a new perspective on what is important in life and with a deeper enjoyment of life. Her story is compelling, written in a wonderfully accessible style and the overwhelming sense is that this book has been written with the sole purpose of making the cancer journey easier for the 'next person'.

Medical science continues to advance. New treatments for cancer are emerging every year and I truly believe that in our lifetime real progress will be made in the 'War on Cancer'. We certainly do not have all the answers in conventional medicine and I entirely support the view that cancer treatment should have a more holistic approach; whether it be relaxation techniques, yoga, religion/spirituality or good, old-fashioned friendship and fresh air, healing for the mind must accompany healing for the body. I urge you to read *A Peaceful Mind*, learn from it, enjoy it and know that the skills that will help you to cope are within your reach.

Dr. Paula Calvert
Consultant Medical Oncologist
Waterford Regional Hospital

Acknowledgments

IT WOULD BE IMPOSSIBLE for me to name everyone who has helped me since my breast cancer diagnosis in June 2000. To all of you...what can I say? Words will never be enough to convey my appreciation.

My friends. I am truly blessed to have you all in my life. Thanks for listening; I know I have a habit of going on... and on! Do you know what; someday we will sort out the world!

My family, especially my sister **Una**...your unending support has been constant and unwavering.

Michael. While I have been indulging myself in allsorts of wonderful therapies and mad ideas you have been there keeping it all together. You are a wonderful father and husband and we all love you very much.

Eoin, Niall, and **Mary.** Can't believe you are all grown up now. We have a lifetime of precious memories. Thanks Eoin for all the help on the computer.

George and **Kathleen MacDonald.** For all the advice, support, editing, photos.

Andrew Delany, Publisher Original Writing.

All the medical and nursing staff in **Waterford Regional**

and **Wexford General Hospital.** You all do an amazing job every day.

Seamus O Reilly, Consultant Oncologist who looked after me brilliantly when I was first diagnosed. Cork is lucky to have you.

Paula Calvert, Consultant Oncologist who took up where he left off and does a wonderful job keeping us all alive.

Finally, but most importantly I want to pay a special tribute to our former family doctor who sadly passed away in April 2005. Doctor **Colin Mitchell** was the first person I contacted when I found my breast lump and as usual he looked after me in his usual professional, kind and gentle way. He was our family doctor since we moved to Gorey in 1984 and I know I speak for many of his patients when I say that we were privileged to have him look after us all so well. May he rest in peace.

My Sponsors
Roche Products Limited Ireland.
Irish Permanent Gorey.
Sheehan Insurance Gorey.
Heiton Buckley Gorey.

Introduction

IN JUNE 2000 I was diagnosed with a stage three aggressive breast cancer. It was without doubt the most powerful wake up call ever to come my way. Following a mastectomy and nine sessions of chemotherapy I now remain cancer free, healthy and well. It really was my worst fear come to pass but thankfully I saw it for what it was...a very loud insistent and unwanted wake up call that I managed over time with a little bit of kicking and screaming to acknowledge, listen to and accept. In that listening I learned so much about myself, about life and what was really important on this topsy turvey journey that is ours. I learned that life doesn't always go to plan, in fact it really can be a right old bitch at times. Whatever happens we have to deal with it and get on as best we know how. I learned that we are all made up of good and bad, positive and negative, we need to work on the negative and find the very best in ourselves and so live life in a way that is authentically our right. Through my illness I learned the bittersweet joy of waking up feeling good after days of feeling terrible, the absolute pleasure of feeling energetic enough to walk on the beach after days of constant exhaustion from all the chemo. The realisation of how good it was to be able to laugh and smile after facing the darkest of moods where there seemed to be nothing to ever smile about again. Above all and most importantly I learned how our thought process plays a very big and important part in our health and well being and when it comes right down to it, we alone have to live and deal with those thoughts. So along with my conventional treatment I set out on my own very personal journey. A journey to find that peaceful mind which would enhance my physical healing, and also enable me to live my life between hospital visit's as normal and worry free as I could. This searching gave me back a wonderful feeling of empowerment and hope where there had been a lot of negativity and hopelessness. So out of the very worst fear came the very best and greatest learning, and that learning goes on and on.

As I started to learn I had a compelling urge to share my newfound philosophies about life with everyone that came my way. You see I needed an outlet for all my thoughts and of course I do know that for a while I drove a lot of those people quite mad with my rather obsessive interest in such things as meditation classes, visualisation, yoga and numerous other therapies of different sorts. I suppose I was feeling the benefit's so much that I just wanted the whole world to know. But I eventually came to the realisation that not everyone wanted to hear what I had to say; mainly due to the rather blank looks and frequent yawns I was receiving when I rambled on and on. I soon realised that my journey was indeed a very personal one and there was no need to try and change everyone around me to my way of thinking. I became rather quiet when I discovered a new way to get it all off my chest. Writing it all down proved to be wonderfully cathartic for me, and so became part of my daily routine. This writing started off first and foremost as a form of healing for myself, an acknowledgment of what I was experiencing i.e. the good and the bad. I had no real structure to it; just a huge need to express it all in some way and get it out of my system. I did after all have so much to say! Over time it slowly grew, gradually becoming more structured and so, slowly and painstakingly, it developed into a book that I hope will be beneficial to anyone who reads it, as it was to me the writer. I have never written a book before so I was going along trusting my instinct, and as I was getting so much satisfaction from the whole experience I continued following my instinct, not knowing where it would take me but trusting that I was doing right.

Now you may say why on earth would anyone want to read a book about the ups and downs of someone's cancer experience, you may even say "now that's really very negative." Well bear with me while I explain why I think differently. We are living in a world that wants to deny anything that is bad, but by doing this we are denying the harsh reality of a very big part of our lives. We need to accept and face the good, the bad, and the ugly times that we all experience. As more of us are honest in sharing these experiences it makes it so much easier for others to do likewise. So the pressure is then taken off us all to appear as if we have to portray a certain "stiff upper lip" image to the world, while all the time we are crying tears inside. It took me awhile to let my guard down and express my deepest fears and this process was made so much easier as a result of the wonderful people I met who shared their feelings with me. In their sharing I was able to realise that I wasn't as alone as I thought and I wasn't going insane. In fact my fears and concerns were perfectly normal, so their honesty made it easy for me to say out loud how I was really feeling. When we hold on to all these dark thoughts the feelings of isolation grow and grow and we feel truly alone, so our healing process is slowed down and our minds cannot be at peace. As I share my story with you I do hope it will allow you to recognise and acknowledge your fears so your healing can truly begin.

My search for wellness and peace took me to various therapists/healers/workshops. A lot of this searching took a lot of time and energy that I didn't always have. My journey took me in many directions that ultimately went full circle and brought me right back to myself. To the realisation of my own strengths, my will to survive and my ability to heal myself in the deepest way possible. An ability that we all have, I might add, but often don't realise. In all that searching I can now say that I found my true self all over again and have learned to look at life in a new more open way. So you see in my writing I am not offering or suggesting anything new...just a reminder of what we all have but sometimes lose sight of. Hopefully, then by reading my experience I will make it easier for you to be reminded of your own inner strengths that are uniquely yours, and to tap into your own innate healing qualities without having to travel the long way round like me.

Whatever stage of life you are at I hope you will allow me to take your hand so you can walk some of the steps of my journey with me, a journey that I feel compelled to share, a journey of sadness and tears, fears worries and laughter, indeed every emotion that it is possible to experience when you stumble blindly along the rocky road of serious illness. A journey that may seem tedious, boring, long and depressing but as you read hopefully you will come to the realisation that by experiencing these emotions there really is light at the end of the tunnel. As we come through the darkness there is a great and beautiful world there to be lived in, a world where we can smile, be happy and be sad. Where it is okay to say that "yes I feel like shit," and by saying it we can then really smile and say "YES I AM POSITIVE" and really really mean it.

I have tried to be as honest and open as possible about my experience. Part one is my cancer experience...my "get well" story. Part two is a combination of different chapters about therapies I found most beneficial to me and are written purely from the perspective of being a cancer patient. It also has individual chapters about various thoughts and emotions and generally ways that I managed to find the peace I craved and needed. So you see you don't have to read it all at once, you can be your own judge of how little or how much you want to read. I do hope though that you will find something in these pages that will help and inspire you to begin your own healing journey and live your life in a way that is your right as a human being. When you awaken each day you know and appreciate the wonderful gift you have been given once again...the amazing wonderful and glorious gift of life. As you acknowledge this over and over again you will realise that the more fully and authentically you live your life the more alive you will feel. It is good to have the courage to look at life in a new way...perhaps not exactly new but in the way you were always meant to see things but along the way it all got a little hazy in all the confusion. If you are prepared to acknowledge change don't be afraid just allow it to unfold. There's no need to force it or try too hard, be gentle and kind to yourself and in that gentleness your soul will be your constant guide. As you awaken to your soul you will know to keep that sense of soul alive and everything really will be okay.

Working as a nurse and massage therapist is a privilege.

I have seen so many people when faced with a crisis find inner strength they never knew they had. They have used their crisis as a time to learn and change, which can often lead them in a whole new direction and way of thinking. This change can be difficult but once you start you know there is no other way. You will also know that the only person you can change is yourself but by doing so it really does affect those around you, as they too begin to look at themselves maybe in a new way also. It is lovely to meet people who are on their own path of discovery and learning, taking small steps, on a journey they often don't know where it is taking them. As more and more people become open to this learning, the world will truly be a much better place to live in, because by finding our own inner peace it automatically spreads to others and so the circle continues.

It is now over seven years since my original diagnosis. When I set out to explore the whole world of complimentary therapy I had no real plan in mind, just an overwhelming need to survive and to enhance the wonderful treatment I was receiving from the medical world that I was so familiar with. I was totally confident that the world I had inhabited as a nurse would look after me well. But, as I said earlier, I could see there were no signposts as to how to cope between hospital visit's, to cope with the turmoil and fear that invaded my mind and had taken me over. So I started my own search, finding ways to harness my healing and create my own peace. As I trawled through numerous books, therapists and workshops I discovered a lot of wonderful but sometimes-weird ideas out there. Thankfully my nursing background kept me grounded, and from being led astray by some rather questionable promises of cures and healings. At a time in our lives when we when we seek help, we are often very vulnerable and so our judgment can become misguided and often blinded in our search for support. I have a great respect for the whole area of complimentary medicine, but unfortunately it does not have the same structures in place as conventional medicine. **I cannot emphasise enough just how important it is to seek medical advice before trying out any type of alternative or complimentary therapy, especially when there is a pre existing medical condition. It is equally as important to ensure that you only choose therapists who are properly qualified in their chosen field.** It is reassuring now that we have more and more cancer support centres in the country. I work in the Hope Support Centre in Enniscorthy Co Wexford and it goes without saying that anyone who avails of centres such as this will be professionally looked after and supported. The best way to find a centre near you is to contact the Irish Cancer Society.

I finished this book in late 2005. On a final note in September 2006 I had breast reconstruction. It wasn't something I had ever considered, but a chance meeting with someone I barely knew who had just had surgery changed my mind. She was so happy with the result that she had no qualms about showing it to me and I was definitely impressed. So thanks to the excellent work of Mr Tadros in Wexford General hospital I am not only balanced in mind body and soul [well I think I am] but I am also a perfectly balanced B cup!

Enjoy!

Everything that happens to you is your teacher. The secret is to learn to sit at the feet of your own life and be taught by it. Everything that happens is either a blessing, which is also a lesson, or a lesson which is also a blessing.

Polly Berrien Berends

Part One

If the future seems overwhelming, remember that it comes one moment at a time.

Beth Mende Conny

Chapter One

WHEN I WAS TOLD THAT I HAD BREAST CANCER I thought I was going to die, maybe not there and then but it certainly seemed like a very real possibility. Now when you are faced with that reality you soon realise how unimportant everything that you have identified yourself is, by this I mean all the external roles you have established in your life. You can no longer be the banker/doctor/nurse or builder because as you confront your mortality you are stripped bare of all these roles. And so you come face to face with who you really are i.e. the real authentic you that has been hidden behind your status in life. We come into the world as pure uncomplicated beings and that's the part of us that continues on when we die, the part of us that has always been there. We just need to rekindle it and return to that authenticity and so get to know ourselves all over again. Faced with the possibility of death that's exactly what I did.

I was 41 when I found my breast lump and while I was stunned and shocked there was a part of me that wasn't too surprised. You see deep inside us all we know when we are doing right or wrong but we choose to ignore those little voices because simply we don't want to listen, and we just don't know how to stop doing what we have always done. At 41 I was busy carrying out my numerous roles as wife, mother and nurse and I am happy to admit that I was a right old fuss pot. I still am mind you, but at least now I know and recognise it and so I know when to cop on to myself when I get a bit carried away with all sorts of nonsense. Of course it took a serious illness for me to finally sit up and listen.

I found my lump on my last day at work before our much awaited and looked forward holiday in France. I had been feeling generally tired for quite awhile mainly because I was constantly on the go giving 100% to everything I did both at work and at home. I subconsciously took on problems and somewhere in my mind I felt I had to make the whole world happy and fix everything for everybody. As a result I was stretching myself too far on a constant basis, which over time was gradually wearing me down. Nobody at home or at work was putting pressure on me to be like this. It was all coming from myself and my way of thinking so I'm not looking for sympathy, just stating a fact. As well as being my personality I believe it was also part of the mind set instilled in us all while training as nurses in the seventies. This mind set meant that we were trained to care for everyone else except ourselves and as a result we were never meant to get sick. So on and on I kept going and there was no talking to me because I didn't want to listen. But then again I portrayed an image to the world of being in control and able to cope with whatever came my way. Having created and built up this image it was then harder to acknowledge any sign of weakness, such as learning to say no which of course would have helped me get off the roller coaster that I was on at that time.

I've come to the conclusion that it is seldom the big things that cause ongoing stress to our nervous system. As human beings we are able to tap into amazing reserves of energy when faced with a crisis or emergency of any sort. It's a collection of little things that get to us and wear us down slowly day-by-day. Now I'm talking about the little things that have the ability to drain our energy supply without us even noticing that it's happening. Little things like deadlines, missed appointments, traffic jams to name but a few. If we don't learn to bring some sense of balance to our time and energy on a daily basis we are constantly on edge. You see a combination of seemingly minor irritants build on each other over time leaving us in a permanent state of tension. This tension eventually catches up with us and manifests it'self in some way usually in the form of a physical illness of some sort.

This seemed to be the way my life was going so I was looking forward to a well-earned rest. Mind you in my tired state that was even a bit of a headache as packing had to be organised which seemed like a major chore because once again I liked it done my way. God but I really was a right old bore, wasn't I! We decided to relax that evening with a bottle of wine so I had a quick shower, slipped on a tracksuit anticipating a nice easy evening with the help of a lovely glass of wine. Can I say here that the whole cancer experience has heightened my awareness of little moments that I wouldn't otherwise have noticed, moments and times that I couldn't ignore where I have felt that someone was helping and guiding me. Now the sceptic in you may think differently but I can only speak from my own experience and my belief, which remains unchanged to this day. That evening was one such moment because for no apparent reason while standing in my sitting room I put my hand on my right breast directly over a very large lump. My first immediate thought was, "I'm going to France next week what on earth am I going to do about this." My anxiety was more to do with the inconvenience of it interfering with my holiday than the fact that it might be cancer. On the other hand a part of me was thinking what would I have done if I was already in France when I found it. At least I was still in my own home where I still had some control and so I knew where to go for help. Some of you may say that you would ignore it until your holiday was over but I couldn't do that. I suppose the nurse in me knew I had to deal with it there and then and thankfully I did especially when I realised later just how very aggressive it was. Time seemed to freeze and as if in slow motion, I remember foolishly thinking maybe it would disappear by tomorrow; so as it was late in the evening I had no choice but to wait until the next day to have it looked at.

After a sleepless night [even with the wine I might add] Michael and myself were first at our doctor's surgery that Saturday morning. I certainly presented him with a dilemma—he was greeted by me saying "we're going to France in a few days, I've found a lump and I want to know what it is before I go on my holiday." I started his day off with a bang but in his usual professional and caring manner he managed to calm me down and organise things as quickly as possible. Because of the whole holiday scenario everything was fast-forwarded very quickly. I was seen that same day by a surgeon in our nearest hospital where he arranged to do a biopsy on the following Monday. In the normal run of events things wouldn't have moved quite so fast but I for one was glad to be doing something so quickly. I still wanted to have our holiday and in my naivety I felt that if I knew what I was dealing with we could still go and whatever needed to be done could wait until we came back. Well, I was certainly proved wrong! Things went as planned and I had the biopsy. I went through the motions of packing for our holiday, which seemed very strange and surreal, but it kept me busy and possibly kept me sane. I can see now that when we are in the middle of something so serious we have the ability to block out the reality of it all just to survive. Denial really has it's uses and can be a great form of protection when we most need it. It doesn't last forever though.

In the meantime the day before our holiday arrived and we were all set to go. My plan was to ring from France for whatever the news would be but as my surgeon was already suspicious he decided to ring for the results, which of course confirmed that it was malignant. He then phoned my husband Michael with the news who had the God-awful task of having to tell me. As I said earlier about my awareness of little moments this was clearly evident once more. You see if I hadn't found my lump when I did I could have been faced with the scenario of finding it on holiday and not knowing what to do about it. On the other hand I could have gone ahead without knowing the results of the biopsy. Now judging by the way I reacted when I was told how aggressive it was, that would have been a nightmare as at peak holiday time it wouldn't have been that easy to turn around and get a flight home. As soon as I knew what I was dealing with I wanted it removed and as it was so aggressive I sincerely believe that if there had been a delay, because of the holiday, I wouldn't be alive today. A friend of mine who experienced serious illness in her family described the whole process as a soap opera. You are on the outside looking in at the drama unfolding knowing somewhere in the back of your mind that you are the main star! You have absolutely no control over what is going to happen next; it's happening but you are not really in tune with yourself. The expression "he was beside himself with worry" is so very appropriate because it was as though I had stepped outside of myself for a while. Do you know what, I never realised just how relevant all those sayings really are to everyday events and happenings but then again I wasn't taking much notice before.

Our own little soap opera continued in our garden as I cooked dinner on the barbecue only to be interrupted by Michael who didn't have to say anything such was the expression on his face. In that timeless few moments it was as though there was no one else in the world but us, it remains frozen in time and was such a strange experience that I find it hard to put into words. All I can say is that time really did stand still, and so I had to physically shake myself into action and knowing that I had a malignant lump growing inside me I wanted it removed as quickly as possible. All thoughts of our holiday were certainly gone out the window. Speaking with the surgeon by phone I was delighted when he organised to have me admitted the next day. I was so glad that things were moving so fast and in the space of a very short time I went through a whole range of emotions from initial uncertainty to terror at the news and then delight when I was told I was going to be dealt with so fast. I think I was slowly cracking up.

We had no choice but to be honest with our children as we had to cancel or holiday. In that moment I felt I was letting everyone down because of this bloody cancer growing in my breast. We never want to consciously hurt our children and their tears that evening left me feeling totally helpless as a parent as I had absolutely no control over what was happening and I couldn't fix and make it better there and then. Maybe we do try to protect our children too much because in the face of a crisis they can and did show a strength and resilience that I hadn't noticed before. They all reacted in their own way and accepted the cancelled holiday quite easily, straight away planning to spend their holiday money on something else...oh the joy and innocence of youth. They were Eoin aged 15, Niall 13, and Mary 10 respectively, and being honest with them was the best thing we could have done. Throughout my illness they were kept informed as to what was happening and that knowledge took a certain amount of the fear away. The fear of wondering what is going on and what's wrong can be more stressful as ones imagination can run wild. As parents we did our best to be as open and honest as possible. When we went through each stage they usually knew beforehand what was going to happen next. When I was sick from the chemotherapy they knew it was the treatment and not the cancer that was making me ill. Cancer has been a part of our lives whether we like it or not. It is not however a constant presence in our day-to-day routine. There was a time in the early stages where everyone at home was being nice to me so I could get away with all sorts. I only had to make a sad face and everyone danced attention on me. That's long gone though and I now get the usual tantrums and moods as any parent does. I must say I wouldn't want it any other way.

As I unpacked our holiday luggage I repacked another bag for my hospital visit. Thursday came which should have been the start of our holiday but instead of heading for the boat we travelled the same road but with a totally different destination. I was totally focussed on one thing, getting to the hospital as quick as possible and getting the surgery over. I appeared controlled focussed and determined on one hand while inside I felt I was hanging on by my fingernails and if I stopped I would fall down into a bottomless pit.

One cannot get through life without pain... What we can do is choose how to use the pain life presents us.

Bernie S. Siegal

Chapter Two

HAVING STAYED IN CONTROL for so long, as soon as I arrived at the hospital admissions desk I seemed to realise the enormity of what was happening and so I just fell apart. I seemed to just give in to this realisation and once the tears started they really flowed and would not stop. I was beyond consolation, and the hard reality of what was happening was staring me in the face. I gradually began to calm down, much to the support and help shown to me by the nurses on duty. Suddenly I was catapulted from being the carer to being a patient, all in the space of a few days. All my years in the profession didn't make one bit of difference. At that time I was just a vulnerable terrified person in need of some help and compassion. My thoughts were running wild and I needed someone to just slow me down and get me to deal with that moment, at that time. Thankfully I got that support, and I haven't forgotten that evening or the people I met who were so wonderful to me. Nurses, or indeed anyone in the medical profession, should never lose sight of how much they affect people they come in contact with. It can be hard, on a busy day to be continuously kind to everyone, but it's good to remember how they deal with someone for admission to hospital can have a hugely positive or negative effect on that person. I do know they are dealing with these crises on a daily basis. However, for the person who is sick it's possibly a first time experience, and so everything that is said and done has a lasting impression that remains with them in a good or bad way. Thankfully, that evening I was shown nothing only kindness and compassion and this continued to be my experience throughout all my care.

When I calmed down, I was still racing ahead in my mind, looking at all the possibilities that could lie ahead for me. I was thinking, chemotherapy, hair loss, sickness, and many other scenarios that were just too scary by far. I had been to the hairdresser a few days earlier, having my hair cut and highlighted, and in a moment of madness I thought "what a waste of money," especially now as I was faced with the chance of losing it all. I was certainly running wild inside my head!! Another insane moment that evening was when my dear friend Mary came to see me. We discussed my possible hair loss, and the fact that I would have to get a wig. She suggested that I should go for a whole new look and try for a Tina Turner wig! Again pure madness, but we still managed a laugh with a slight hysteria attached I might add.

My surgeon came to see me and we discussed my planned surgery for the next day. I was adamant that I wanted a full mastectomy, and even suggested that he could remove both if it meant a better chance for me to survive. I know that the survival rate is the same, whether one has a lump removed, or a total mastectomy, but because my lump seemed to be so big, I just wanted it all gone. When you are faced with the possibility of losing your life, losing a breast seems like a small price to pay to save yourself. He discussed all options with me, but I had my mind made up—and so the consent form was signed. I eventually settled down, hopefully to get some sleep, as there was nothing else left for me to do. The hospital had taken on an air of quiet, visitors were gone home and patients settled down for the night as nurses did their nightly rounds. In this silence I felt truly alone and in that solitude I realised that no matter who was with me, at the end of the day I had to ultimately face this on my own.

Okay, so I had every support possible from my family and friends but the reality was this cancer was mine and mine alone. Your doctor can close your chart, put it away and go home. Your cancer only affects him when he is sitting in front of you and that's the way it should be. He can't take your fears and worries with him when he leaves, if he did he wouldn't be able to continue working as a doctor help-ing people. He would end up getting sick himself. It's your illness, you alone wake up with it, go to sleep with it, walk into the doctor's surgery with it, and it's still with you when you walk out. It's with you all the time and the very thought of that can drive you crazy if you don't try and deal with it in some way. There really is no such thing as running away from it. You can pretend that it isn't happening by keeping constantly busy but it doesn't go away no matter how deeply you bury it in your thoughts. As soon as you start to deal with it, that's when you begin to heal. Sometimes this will happen straight away in a crisis, but it may be months or even years, before you are ready to confront what has hap-pened. There are no rules, you yourself will know when.

I felt a certain peace in being alone, even though I was terrified. My tears had all dried up and the sadness I was feeling was so deep that it couldn't, at that time, be relieved by any amount of tears. It was just good to be on my own and try and unravel my thoughts. The need to be at peace with myself became the ultimate part of my healing journey. Everything I write about in this book is my way of enhancing that feeling through learning to be content in my own company. I love to talk, but we all need time alone and being silent I'm not saying that we should run away to a monastery!! Just find moments of quiet and peace in our day-to-day lives, helping us to look deep inside ourselves and so finding our own healing strength.

My surgery went as planned and Michael was there with me when I woke up. I remember in my fuzzy post anaesthetic state being able to feel a certain relief that the lump was gone and it was all over. I recovered well physically and I was anxious to have a look at my scar as soon as possible. While I was terrified and dreaded what my reaction would be it wasn't as bad as I thought and thanks to the nursing staff I was given a temporary prosthesis, which made me look half normal at least! Learning to accept the loss of my breast played a major part in my healing process. Some women find the experience deeply traumatic, and I think it depends on how we feel about ourselves and where we are at in our lives, i.e., married, single, young, old.

A mastectomy is without doubt a life-changing event and takes time and a lot of soul searching to get used to it. I believe a lot of healing can happen if we choose to see beyond the actual physical body and our outer physical appearance, to dig deeper and see what being a woman means to us. It most definitely isn't just about our breasts and certainly isn't something that a surgeon can just cut away. If, however, we continuously tell ourselves that we are scarred for life to the point where we will never feel whole again, we are denying ourselves the chance to really see how we value ourselves as women. By having the courage to dig deep and look inwards we discover so many things about ourselves. Good and positive things that come together to make up the real "us." Our confidence grows and we become more and more aware that there is so much more to being a woman than being obsessively attached to our outer physical appearance. It can be an opportunity in disguise to grow and learn as human beings and isn't that why we are here in the first place?

I can honestly say that losing a breast has not been too traumatic for me. Yes, I have shed many tears looking at the place where my breast use to be. I do often still avoid looking at the scar. If, on a bad day I'm full of self-pity I remind myself of how privileged I am to be alive and well and how much the whole experience has changed me for the better and taught me so much. Wearing a prosthesis can have it's awkward moments, though! I chose not to have breast reconstruction so I now wear one of these, which means I have to buy special bras and swimming togs that have a pouch to hold it in place. These can only be bought in specialised shops and I do miss not being able to just walk into a department store and buy them over the counter. Thankfully Marks and Spencer's have taken the initiative and are stocking a great range of post surgery bras. Going swimming can have it's moments, especially if the changing rooms are communal. Trying to get my prosthesis from my bra into my swimming togs can be awkward at times. Sometimes when I get out of the pool my prosthesis has slipped down slightly in it's pouch, and I can look lopsided! I refuse to let these things stop me from doing the things I love. Okay, it was hard the first few times, but the quicker I did it after surgery, the easier it was for me. We seem to think that all eyes are on us in these situations, but really they are not. People are usually too busy wondering how they are looking themselves to really notice you! Once I am comfortable that's all that matters. Swimming is one of the really good things that has helped me to develop a positive body image about myself. I always feel so well and energetic after being in the pool that it helps to give my confidence a much-needed boost. By doing this I don't allow insecurities and negative thoughts to take over. Again as I said earlier it's about choices, will I go swimming and feel great? or will I not go and feel sorry for myself? By not going I'm allowing the cancer to take over. I do have to consciously talk myself into going some days, but once I make the decision to go I start feeling better straight away. Following my chemotherapy and subsequent Tamoxofin medication I have gained quite a bit of weight. I don't like it very much but again I remind myself of the privilege it is to be alive and well and I am just too stubborn and pig-headed to let it stop me from leading my life

My time in hospital was a roller coaster of emotions. Mainly I was quite "high" from all the care and attention that was being showered on me by friends, family and hospital staff. I was carried along from day to day on a wave of support and rarely had a chance to be alone. When I was alone, I often shed tears that seemed to rise up from somewhere deep inside me; it was as though my whole body was crying with the sadness of it all. It was such a release to do this and often when in the shower I would let the tears flow and talk out loud to my mother, father and sister Mary (all deceased) or indeed anyone that I thought could help me. I'm sure anyone passing by often thought I was quite mad because this was a regular occurrence...and sure maybe I was! I still have a tendency to talk out loud to myself when I am alone. Sometimes I forget though and I'm sure the neighbours have often heard me talking to my two dogs but they are well used to me by now. My world in hospital became very small; nothing outside the four walls seemed real anymore. I know that my family and friends were dealing with the reality of it all whereas I was in a cocoon of being cared for and looked after. A part of me started to dread going home, as I knew I would have to face the real world again. This really says a lot about my way of thinking at the time, as I was normally the type who thought our home would fall apart if I wasn't in it! I can see how easy it is to become institutionalised when one is in any hospital or prison for too long. It's amazing how quickly my view of the world changed. I was only in hospital for two weeks and yet it very quickly became like the only world I had ever known.

Michael, Eoin, Niall and Mary came in to see me often. The first time they were all with me after my operation I remember feeling utterly content and happy that all I wanted in my life was here with me. Now this probably sounds really corny to you. But, you see from where I was at that point nothing beyond that moment seemed important, just us as a family together. It was like one of those moments frozen in time where everything is crystal clear, where I knew how unimportant all the material trappings of life were to me. I was being shown what really was essential and I could see that anything outside that room meant nothing. To this day I remind myself of that thought, especially when I'm on a rampage trying to clean my house or get something new or of course when we are all driving each other mad. It's good to stop and remind ourselves daily what's important, we are all only human, and we will still moan and groan, and wish we could win the lotto! But as long as we keep our feet on the ground and every so often remind ourselves of our priorities, then we will be less likely to go mad when the dog eats our Sunday dinner!

Subsequent scans all came back clear and so Michael and I met with Seamus O'Reilly, the Oncologist, to discuss my cancer and my treatment. I can still remember every moment of that meeting, and the feelings I had. Seamus O'Reilly is one of life's true gentlemen and gives bad news in the best way possible. He looked after me so well and when I was finished all of my chemo he moved to Cork to take up a new position. Of course I was sorry to see him go but thankfully his replacement Dr Paula Calvert continues to look after me just as well. I do send Seamus an annual Christmas card just to remind him of the great job he did in helping me on the road to recovery...But back to that day, I wanted to know everything about my lump even though I was absolutely terrified of what he would say. I felt I just had to know, because if not the fear of not knowing would drive me insane anyway. I thought, "I'll ask everything and deal with it somehow." I was feeling physically weak with fear, and only for Michael's actual physical presence I think I'd have fallen off the chair, as my body seemed lifeless and drained of energy. My lump was big and nasty but on a positive note (and boy was I grasping at anything that would give me hope), only one lymph gland showed signs of cancer and my remaining breast and all my scans were clear. I was beginning to think that maybe I had chance after all.

My chemotherapy was planned for six weeks later to allow my body heal following surgery. I was asked to volunteer for a clinical trial and of course I jumped at the chance, as I was willing to take anything that was being offered no matter what it entailed. Clinical trials are conducted in hospitals as a way to try out new drugs or new ways of giving them. The trial was called "The Big Trial," because of the large numbers taking part in it around the country. However I did not know that, and I used to wonder why it was called "The Big Trial" but I never thought to ask. As I was a suitable candidate for this trial, I thought maybe it's for big women only! Or maybe it's for women with big breasts!

I was definitely going slightly insane with the most amazing things popping up inside my head on a daily basis.

The night before I left hospital for home I dreamt about my sister Mary who died from a congenital heart disease aged 17, when I was 7. In the dream she came to see me, and I was so excited to see her, so of course I wanted her to meet Michael, Eoin, Niall and Mary. She said, " but I've only come to see you." In the dream she appeared as the age she would have been if alive, i.e. ten years older than me. How do I know this, I can't really explain, only to say I had a sense of her being older than me. The dream ended there, as I was woken by the staff bringing in my breakfast. I didn't think too much about it at the time, in fact I was inclined to blame it on wishful thinking or a combination of medications I was taking. However, as I said at the beginning of this book about my life since my illness being full of coincidences and unexplained moments, this again proved to be one such moment.

When dates were being arranged for my chemotherapy they were changed a few times and eventually August 16th was given to me as my starting date. This date is the anniversary of my sister Mary's death so I certainly felt like I was being given a clear message of being looked after. There are no scientific answers to it and remember now I was rather sceptical of things like this before my illness. I do believe I was being made aware that I was being cared for; in fact I honestly believe I was been given a very clear message. Once again, as I said earlier, you might think "here she goes again" but I now know and accept that we only have to ask for guidance and help and we will get it. Unfortunately, in our busy noisy world, we miss and don't notice these lovely little moments that are often the most significant. I also experienced a great sense of peace and strength from the many people who were praying for me, sending me cards and inspiring letters. It can only be good to have so many people thinking such nice thoughts about you. I now believe and understand what the power of prayer really means and I will never underestimate it's power.

I headed for home, which for a while didn't feel like my home. For a start my sister Una, had gone mad cleaning and polishing, buying new bed linen and all sorts. The children enjoyed telling me about the fun they had slipping and sliding over the hall floor because never before was it so shiny from all the polish! Again this was Una's way of helping me, and I love her dearly for it. She continued to come down at weekends all through my chemotherapy, usually laden down with lots of lovely things for my freezer and generally providing us with endless support, love and much needed help. Eventually I settled in and home started feeling like mine again and it was so good to be in my own place once more. You see, when all is said and done there really is no place like it.

Be mindful of how you approach time. Watching the clock is not the same as watching the sun rise.

Chapter Three

THE PERIOD BETWEEN MY HOSPITAL DISCHARGE and start of my chemotherapy was about six weeks in total. It was a strange time of mixed emotions, and had an overall feeling of unreality about it. Schools were closed, so our children were on their holidays, and what with numerous family and friends coming to visit, I was rarely alone. It was lovely chatting to old friends, and I was having quite a good time being made a fuss of! At the back of my mind I knew though that there were a lot of dark thoughts just waiting to come to the surface, but I was quite happy to keep busy and just not think too much. However, I couldn't keep busy constantly so when I was alone there was no running away from what was going on inside my head. Outwardly, I looked okay and people would say, "you're looking great," but inside my head was another story entirely. Never before was I so aware of what was going on in my thought process. There was just no running away from them, no matter whom I was with, or what I was doing; they nibbled away at the edge of my consciousness. Mornings were usually the worst, as my first thought on waking would be "I have cancer." It was like facing it for the first time every time I woke up. I'd wallow in the sadness of it all for a while and then I'd put it away and face the day.

I didn't want to say out loud how I was feeling, as I didn't want to upset Michael or any of my family. They in turn, had their fears, but didn't want to upset me by voicing them. So we were all busy minding each other, but I was left still carrying around a lot of negative thoughts inside my head. With no particular plan in mind I started to write down my feelings, especially on very bad days. I would rant and rave on paper to my heart's content, knowing no one would read it, so I could say what I liked. I felt totally safe just letting it all out. I wasn't ready to talk openly to anyone just then, as I was feeling very vulnerable, so it was a great way to start. It's similar to our school days, when a diary gave us the freedom to write our deepest thoughts safe in the knowledge that no one would see it! No one certainly saw what I wrote and I never reread it. I continued to do this right throughout my treatment and it was a wonderful source of healing for me. I kept it hidden and three years later when I started counselling, I took it out into the garden along with my wig and set them both alight. I felt like doing some kind of tribal dance as they went up in flames. It was as though I was moving on to a new stage in my life. It really was such a good feeling...I decided against the dance just in case any of the neighbours were watching!

It is hard to voice our thoughts, because by saying them out loud we are making them real. We try and keep going because the fear is, that once we start, we won't be able to get up and go again. These thoughts won't go away though, so at least by writing them down we are being gentle with ourselves and getting rid of some of the emotional baggage that causes us so much heartache and stress. I spoke with a lady who had lost her husband about five years earlier. She had children to rear and felt that only then all those years later, could she begin to confront her grief. She had to keep going at the time and was just afraid to let go as she felt she wouldn't get up again. She was only then starting to grieve. You see there are no rules, no right or wrong way. Sometimes denial can be a gift as it is a form of protection until we are ready to face whatever it is we are running from. Everybody deals with their own crises in their own time and in a way that is right for them alone. As human beings we should never judge how someone deals with their own situation because their way may not be ours. Ultimately it is their decision to live their lives by what is right for them.

For me the process of dealing with my "crisis" was a very gradual one. Days went by and I'd be fine, and then I'd hit days of utter sadness and grief that left me drained, tense and irritable. I never knew from day to day how I would be feeling and neither did my family, but they copped on fairly quickly and knew the days to stay away from me!! Their antennae became very fine tuned to my moods and they had a fair idea how I was feeling fairly fast. I knew that on a "down" day I was better off just to deal with it as best I could. Trying to act as if I was okay was putting me under more pressure and hence I'd end up feeling worse. With a family to care for it wasn't always possible to remove myself off somewhere but I'd find moments to be alone, or I'd take myself off to bed early and just relax. Doing this meant I'd usually wake up feeling better the next day. Pushing myself too much would leave me overtired and overwhelmed which only increased my sense of helplessness. So I gradually learned the hard way to be as gentle with myself as possible. I was becoming more fine tuned to my thoughts and as I said earlier they can be our greatest enemy causing us endless turmoil, but also they can be and are our greatest teacher and are our most valuable possession. By becoming more in tune with our inner thoughts/voice we discover that we will be guided in a way that is right for us alone. We can choose to let our negative thoughts take over but we can also choose to direct our thoughts in a more positive way. Now I sincerely hope I don't sound like someone who is totally self obsessed, I need to say here that I'm far from being like that. I am more self aware which is a good way to be but it is a long long way from being self obsessed.

In the meantime I had numerous hospital visit's for tests in preparation for my chemotherapy. In my mind I began to have a love-hate relationship with Seamus O'Reilly, my oncologist. I loved the way he dealt with me, always giving me loads of time and answering all my questions, no matter how bizarre they were. On the other hand though, I hated what he represented—cancer. On these visit's I hated sitting in the waiting room surrounded by cancer patients, as I felt I wanted to have nothing to do with them. It was so surreal, only a few weeks earlier I was a nurse, the carer and now I had very quickly become one of them—a statistic. Dates were being arranged for the start of my chemotherapy and were changed a few times before a final date was set. August 16th was to be the day and as I said earlier this was the anniversary of my sister Mary's death. So along with the dream I had about her and now this I felt protected and cared for which gave me a great sense of comfort and peace.

I was also beginning to realise there aren't always scientific answers to everything. Our society today is full of people who need hard facts, surveys and scientific explanations for everything, sure wasn't I one such person. In trying to find out these "scientific answers" the sense of spirituality has become lost. By learning to follow your own heart it will tell you what is feeding your soul and your soul will be your true guiding light. The main thing is to learn to trust your own soul. If you stop and think about it, little things happen to everybody. Everyday little moments that influences a thought or action. Unfortunately, we aren't always aware of these moments as our busy noisy lifestyle doesn't allow us to. Maybe too, we are afraid to believe that there is something beyond our control or understanding or work. Isn't it great then to have the courage to look beyond that and see the deeper reality to our physical selves, a deep sense of spirituality that is our very essence? Someone once said, "we are not physical beings having a spiritual experience but spiritual beings having a physical experience."

Life without this spiritual connection can be a very empty one and to deny it leaves us with something missing from our lives that no material wealth can fulfil. We do not have a spiritual side to our nature, our nature, you see is all-spiritual. I read one of many newspaper articles written about survivors of the September 11th tragedy in New York. One article spoke about many very personal experiences that happened to people on the day. Little things that happened meant they were out of the building when the planes hit. Little things that at the time were a nuisance but I'm sure now they say were a blessing from God. Like the lady who spilled coffee on her suit, she was late because she had to change her clothes. She missed the disaster by minutes, or the office manager who was out of the office buying doughnuts as it was his turn—he survived. Or the gentleman who stopped off at the drugstore for a band-aid for his sore foot and was late for work, so he is alive today. There were many more similar stories and I'm sure all these people are now more aware of the hand of God at work in their daily lives and of how fragile life really is and also how possibly it just wasn't their time. You see it's those fleeting little moments when the most profound events occur in our lives. The thing is though to be aware and learn from these little moments.

The weeks slipped by and I got on with life arranging schoolbooks etc, and just dealing with the daily routine of family life. There were lovely moments as friends and family came to visit often so overall I was having a fairly "okay" time. Big Brother mania had hit our screens for the first time and I was soon hooked! It was great to just lose myself in the silliness of it all. It was easy to lose myself as I sat on my couch drinking coffee, watching other people sit on their couch doing the same thing—drinking coffee!! "How mad is that?" I'd say to myself. So even the most mundane had it's role to play in my getting well. You see, it's a great sense of escapism to read a meaningless mind-numbing book, to watch a similar TV programme and to just forget everything for a while at least. We can't always be too deep and serious, analysing everything. It's good to have fun as well and it's all about balance.

Physically I was feeling very well and anxious to get started on my chemotherapy even though I was terrified. We were in the process of redecorating our sitting room and when we put up the new curtains I remember wondering would I be around when we changed them again. These thoughts sent me off on a total obsession with time. Suddenly I was adding up years, wondering would I be around in two years, five years and so on. For ages I was quite frankly driving myself mad and I knew I had to do something, otherwise not only would I go insane but so too would all those around me. That's when I started talking to myself!...I had daily conversations going on inside my head where I'd say "well, Bernie, even if you hadn't faced cancer how do you know where you'll be next week, next year or even tomorrow, you might get knocked down by a car or run over by a bus?" In the meantime I was also wasting precious moments trying to see ahead and by doing this I wasn't just enjoying the day I had. This constant internal chatter began to have some effect. I started each day by trying very hard to slow myself down thanking God for the gift of a new day and so I began to gradually make a conscious effort to live in the moment I was in. By doing this I started to slow down and just became more aware of little things. As my awareness grew, so too did my appreciation of the value of time. The reality of serious illness was helping me not to focus on the outcome of my illness, but to focus on the daily privilege it was to just be alive and experience the gift of the universe all around me. To walk in the sunlight and beauty of nature makes us realise that the universe is the real timekeeper. As this awareness increased I began to open up to the inner vitality of everything around me. As I slowed down I was paying more attention to each living moment. Waking up to a new day became a gift, the privilege of walking in our very beautiful Courtown woods, or being anywhere close to nature. That lovely feeling of being with those you love and just "being" not doing anything. All simple things but ooh so precious and fulfilling. This awareness required and does require daily reminding and revisiting and is now a part of me that is truly a gift.

But back to me, walking in beautiful places and being in touch with nature is all very well, but real life and it's practicalities have to be dealt with. I don't spend every moment doing this, as I go about my daily life I do have a fairly constant awareness of the bigger picture and of what is and isn't important. In a way it's quite easy to float away on a cloud of spirituality but the real test is all about finding balance between mind, body and spirit. And so in my fairly balanced lifestyle the practicalities had to be dealt with as chemo was drawing near so I headed off with my friend Yvonne and bought a wig—not a Tina Turner style I have to say, but a very sensible style similar to my own. Finally, August 16th arrived and Michael and myself headed off for Waterford Regional Hospital not knowing what to expect but ready for whatever the day brought. "Poor old me," I could have said, but that internal chatter started up again and I thought "let's look at this another way and see what happens" and so I'd say 'why not lucky old me." You may well say why. But you see wasn't I lucky to be given a fighting chance to get well by being offered chemotherapy and if that's what it took, well then I was more than ready for it. This internal chitchat wasn't so bad after all!

When you say, "I have a gut feeling about something" you are not speaking metaphorically, you're speaking literally, because your gut makes the same chemicals as your brain when it thinks.

Deepak Chopra

Chapter Four

SITTING IN THE CHEMOTHERAPY WARD that first day I was struck by the weird sense of normality of it all. There I was, like all those around me, attached to a drip, that was slowly administering a cocktail of drugs, which would hopefully restore us all to good health. We were all in the same situation but I certainly didn't want to be a part of "them." I suppose I hadn't really started to come to terms with the realisation that I was a cancer patient so in my mind I tried to distance myself from them as much as possible. Just a few weeks earlier I was going about my daily life as wife, mother, and nurse, taking the normality of it all for granted. With all my heart and soul I wanted to be one of those nurses on duty that day. Now I've no doubt they were wishing the day over but from where I was sitting the normality of their routine was what I most wished for. I envied them their seemingly carefree day but the harsh reality was staring me in the face, I couldn't run from it, so I looked around me I was a bit taken aback to see all these people having chemo, being quite normal, chatting and just getting on with it.

I mean to say what was I expecting, a room full of people, all totally miserable, all just waiting…all too full of self-pity to talk to each other. I really do believe that in the back of my mind that's what I was thinking. People do interpret the word cancer as a death sentence but I was seeing a different scenario. Okay, everyone had a cancer diagnosis but in the face of this diagnosis no matter how bad it seemed they were getting on with it as best they could. They were surviving, not just existing, but also being as cheerful and upbeat as possible. They all had their own stories and fears but they were doing their best, and the next day would bring another group of people all facing the same thing.

It seemed that everyone had a story to tell and no matter how sad it was, most of them still managed to remain relatively upbeat. It is so easy to be negative when you have a cancer diagnosis and, unfortunately, it is often only the negative stories that we hear. When I began to accept what was happening, to let my guard down and share my own fears I discovered so many people living with cancer. This helped me to put my own worries into context and just knowing that I was not alone was a comfort and gave me much needed reassurance at that time. Believe me, there are many positive and encouraging stories out there. We were all strangers with a common bond forming fleeting friendships that at the time were supportive and warm and so very reassuring and helpful. Mind you not everyone was positive and upbeat. I learned pretty quickly to avoid the very negative people and those who had suddenly become medical experts because of their illness. It never ceases to amaze me how people are so happy to tell their complete stories to a total stranger, not just their stories but also the most intimate and possibly exaggerated details. Maybe it says a lot about us all and how desperate we are to be heard. I never minded listening but sometimes I needed to protect myself. A good book and Walkman were a nice polite way of avoiding unwanted conversations! Everyone deals with their journey in their own way so I'm not passing judgment and saying they were wrong—I was just choosing to protect myself and avoid negativity. Often it was enough for me to carry myself besides having to carry someone else as well. Sometimes in that room full of strangers, there was no need for conversation anyway as we were all sharing a common bond so we were often happy to be alone with our thoughts.

Cancer really has two sides to it—on one hand it is a terrifying, mind-blowing experience and on the other it intensifies the present like nothing else can. It sharpens and fine-tunes our awareness so we choose to really experience and savour those little moments. So instead of totally dreading each hospital visit as I imagined I would, in a strange way I began to enjoy the opportunity to meet a vast number of people I wouldn't otherwise have met. I was having my chemo in the hospital where I had trained as a nurse, so some of my colleagues from those days would come to see me and we had a chance to catch up on our lives. I shared much laughter and tears and heard many uplifting and inspiring stories from fellow cancer patients. We were all on our own journey affecting each other in different ways, hopefully helping each other to learn to smile, to share friendship no matter how fleeting and temporary it was. To hopefully help each other gain some knowledge, to be positive and above all to get through another hopefully not so bad chemo day. I have never met anyone from my days in the chemo room since and we never arranged to do so. You see it wasn't about making lasting friendships; instead it was one of those fleeting intense moments in time that remains clear and fixed in my mind. The people I met will always be clear in my mind and I do hope they all remain well and happy. By shedding the "poor me" we can find loads of opportunities in even the most difficult situations. We shall never really know as we go through life how many lives ours have touched but we can be sure of one thing, we do all affect each other, be it good or bad. I sincerely hope that everyone I met throughout my treatment was in some small way enriched for having met me, as I was by those I came in contact with.

Before I got sick I was constantly preoccupied with planning and anticipating my future. I seemed to always have a list of things to do. I can now recognize that there was a great deal wrong with the way I had been leading my life. As I said earlier, no one was putting pressure on me to be the world's greatest organizer, it was coming from myself. I was often so busy and pre-occupied that I could eat a meal and not really taste it, walk along a beautiful beach and not really see the beauty all around me. I'm sure you, the reader, if you are totally honest will identify with what I have just said. In fact I will go so far as to say that almost everybody leads their life missing out on a lot of precious moments such is the extent of their busy lifestyle. Isn't it better then to make a conscious decision to, okay, still plan a certain amount but not let it be the force that constantly drives us, controlling our day to day lives, and instead choose to get up each day and live and experience each moment to the full. This conscious decision will intensify our awareness and so we will take pleasure from the smallest things and we really will wake up and "smell the roses." We will gradually stop trying to consciously plan our lives, which really is our way of trying to be in control. Instead pay attention, slow down, make contact with ourselves and connect with the stream of life around us

The in between times were a mixture of good and bad.

While I was learning to appreciate lots of happy moments it wasn't by any means all sunshine. I'd love to say I sailed through it but there were times when I felt absolutely awful and looked even worse. I'd look in the mirror some days at my bloated face and baldhead, and believe me the last thing on my mind would be a positive thought. After all we are only human so it was okay to be miserable and God help anyone who tried preaching positive thinking to me on those days. It was impossible to remain upbeat when I was feeling just so miserable and exhausted. It was really a question of getting through each day as best I knew how.

There certainly wasn't much room for too much analysing life and soul searching, as all my energy was being channelled into dealing with the vast range of symptoms that came with the chemotherapy. The hospital staff gave me prescriptions for various medications to help ease these symptoms and I followed their advice to the full. I wanted to make it as easy as possible and I certainly wasn't going to be a martyr and think I could do it on my own. Yes, I wanted to be in control and I was very open to anything that would enhance my ability to cope with my illness but my main priority was to the conventional treatment being offered, i.e., chemotherapy. I had and still have a huge respect for the accumulated experience of oncologists, doctors and all the medical profession, so I did not want to interfere in any way with my prescribed care. I can't emphasize it enough how important it is to always check with one's medical team before trying out any other therapy or treatment. There is always the danger of being led to believe that a certain therapy will be a total cure and so possibly putting oneself at a greater risk as a person may then choose to abandon their chemotherapy or whatever prescribed treatment they are following. I believe it's about balance and combining both conventional and alternative treatments in a safe and sensible way. It's also about gaining as much knowledge as you need to help you stay in control of what is happening to you.

My hair started to fall out after about two weeks, so instead of watching it slowly come away which was distressing I decided to have it all cut off. I was frightened of losing my hair at first, but I soon got used to my baldhead. I had a wig and numerous bandanas and scarves in various colours, so I became quite good co-ordinating everything to make myself look as best I could. I never really liked wearing my wig but it was a necessity, as my head would get very cold without it. As soon as my hair started to grow I stopped wearing it. I used to think that I looked fairly ok and hadn't changed much but I was proven wrong. I remember when I was nearing the end of my treatment I met my work colleagues for lunch, now some of them hadn't seen me for quite a while and I could see straight away that some of them didn't recognize me. I was getting very good at picking up on peoples expressions and I know it was more embarrassing for them than for me. Of course I had changed in appearance from all the steroids etc so it was inevitable that something like that would happen. At that stage I was beyond caring what people thought and anyway I'd remind myself that it was the inside bit, "me," that was most important. Sometimes though I had to work very hard at finding that inside bit! On a positive note about baldness, apart from all the money saved on hairdressers, time saved on washing and drying, head massage takes on a whole new meaning as there is no hair in the way of those nerve endings which makes the experience truly enjoyable and sensual.

It is so important to be authentically and genuinely yourself, not what others want you to be, or how others think you should behave. We can become bogged down in putting up a front and behaving in a way that people expect us to. This can be made even more difficult in the face of people who mean well but have a cheer leading attitude to everything. So that no matter how bad you say you are feeling they tell you, "you'll be okay." We need to remind ourselves in these situations that the problem is theirs, not ours. If someone we meet has a problem and is uncomfortable around our illness, they need to look at their own fears around the whole area of cancer and all that goes with it. When they say, "it's okay," it's their way of not confronting what is happening, but it is putting us under more pressure to appear constantly happy. I do believe that the more open and honest we are about our feelings, people will stop trying to constantly "rescue" us by trying to "fix" everything and instead just listen and allow us to be miserable if we want to be.

The weeks passed and winter crept in, bringing with it endless rain and floods. As a child I always loved the feeling of being tucked up safe in bed on a miserable wet windy night listening to the rain and wind, feeling safe and snug in the warmth of my bed. So now it was as though the weather was giving me permission to do just that. On my "off" days I would feel a certain contentment lying in bed and in the stillness I would start to indulge in thinking about all sorts, letting fantasy run free, planning world trips and numerous nice things for when I would be well again. There is always a feeling that we should be up and about when the sun is shining and summer is a time when we are most active. Winter is a time to slow down and hibernate, so it was a good time for me to be having chemo as there wasn't much I could do anyway as the weather was so bad. Routine became established in our house for those months. Chemo every three weeks followed by good and bad days. Bad days I would get up and see everyone off to work/school, do a very quick tidy up (fussy days long gone!) and then back to bed, usually until lunch time or so. Lying in bed I was often just too tired to sleep so I'd lie awake mainly feeling sorry for myself wallowing in self-pity and just being miserable. I knew how important it was to be positive. I also knew that hating and resenting what was happening was wasting valuable energy that I needed to fight my illness, sure indeed I knew it all but at times I just didn't care what happened. But once again, as I said earlier, that internal chatter would start which I often felt like ignoring as it would have been easier to stay in the black hole, but it would keep on chattering and so I'd get a glimmer of strength to keep going and in control. I knew that the medical profession were controlling my prescribed care but ultimately only I had control of my attitude. I had the choice as to how to deal with it so I'd have a serious chat with myself and tell myself to "cop on." God! but there were days where I was awful busy talking to myself!

I started listening to classical music and discovered a wonderful way to relax and divert all those awful thoughts. I couldn't do much else lying there and the music became a way to keep me relaxed and allow my mind to just absorb the beautiful sounds, so instead of wallowing in self pity I was carried away on a wave of relaxation. Michael, being forever thoughtful, bought me a clock radio with a built in stereo so it became part of our routine to fall asleep to nice easy music. My collection of classical music grew and continues to be something I love. It is such a simple thing but so very powerful as a means of relaxation. No one was telling me to do this and no one was telling me to write down my thoughts; as I said earlier, I had a strong sense of being constantly guided in the right direction. I had asked for help, and I sincerely believe that we only have to ask and then we only have to learn to listen and I certainly had plenty of time to listen. By learning to trust we will come to realize that there is not one question we can ask that somewhere deep in our souls we do not have the answer to. Once we become conscious of this we will then be guided in a way that is right for us always. The thing is to trust and not ignore our "gut" feeling. I was getting better at listening to my own gut instinct and by doing so gave me a sense of empowerment that made me feel I was doing something for me instead of letting everyone else have control. Without my illness these doctors and drug companies would be out of a job. My illness was helping to pay their salaries so they needed me, but it was up to me how much I needed them and how much control I wanted them to have! I certainly had a lot of conversations going on inside my head and it was probably just as well that I wasn't thinking out loud as my doctor would have started to question my sanity!

The bad days would pass and I would wake up to a new day feeling good. I would acknowledge and give thanks for the feeling of being well and the bad days would quickly be forgotten, as I wouldn't want to waste a minute of a precious good day feeling sorry for myself. Instead I would be out and about enjoying the simplest things like having a coffee and chat with friends and getting carried away with just being well again. Suddenly I had a sharper appreciation of all it meant to just be okay. And people would come up to me and say "you're looking well" and I'd think, "if only they could see inside my head."

It is good to have an end to journey towards, but it is the journey that matters in the end.

Ursula K. LeGuin

Chapter Five

AS THE TIME PASSED my energy levels remained depleted to say the least. Family life continued as normal as possible and only for the practical help from my friends and family, we would probably have starved. They continuously topped up my freezer with prepared meals and home baking which was truly wonderful. You see, no matter what is going on in the world children will still get hungry. Along with that my sister Una arrived down most weekends from Dublin laden down with lots of lovely goodies from Marks And Spencer's and Superquinn. Is it any wonder then that I put on so much weight...I was definitely comfort eating and no matter how sick I felt I still managed to do so—I really do love my food!

I felt overwhelmed at times with the generosity and good-will that was coming my way. To be really honest I found it hard to accept at first. Why? you might ask. Well up to that point I was happier when I was doing things for others. I suppose I found it difficult to accept help. It was certainly easier to be in the giving role than the receiving one. You could say that this is partially to blame from our training as nurses.

In this role we constantly give and care for others. We then become mothers and that giving and caring continues. The problem then is that in a lifetime of giving we totally forget about ourselves. About how to sometimes admit that we are not as strong as we think, that it's ok to be a little bit "self. .ish" once in a while. It is definitely not a sign of weakness to reach out and admit that sometimes we need a little help and support to keep going. Being a little "self...ish" is no harm at all . There certainly is no need to feel any sense of guilt about it. By tending to our own needs we give to others in a much more open way...not because we have to but because we want to. If you think about it there's not much to be gained from constantly giving while all the time ignoring our own needs. We certainly wouldn't let a car run without petrol... it will eventually slow down and stop. The same applies to us humans...running on empty will eventually force us to do the same possibly because of an illness of some sort.

My back was to the wall so I had no choice but to accept all the help that came my way. Letting my barrier down and saying "yes, I need help," was difficult as being told to be positive had the ability to make me feel that I had to keep in control and so show the world that I was coping all on my own. We are only human though and people feel very helpless when faced with our illness. They are delighted to be doing something. For them, feeling useful lessens their feelings of helplessness so when you think about it like that we are really doing them a favour! Outwardly, I seemed to be coping but my thoughts were ever changing and deep down I found it hard to focus on a bright future. I was doing my best, writing in my journal, listening to relaxing music, trying to think positive thoughts but deep down in the recesses of my mind I was really just going through the motions and the fear I was experiencing was all consuming and terrifying.

A Reach to Recovery volunteer from the Irish Cancer Society came to see me when I was in hospital. I continued to have contact by phone with one of these volunteers throughout my treatment and it was a great source of comfort and inspiration for me. These volunteers are people who have recovered from breast cancer, and go on to give their time freely to the Irish Cancer Society, helping others who are newly diagnosed. It was truly a lifeline for me, especially when I was wallowing in self-pity. To be able to talk to someone who had been there, who had gone on to recovery and lead a full life, gave me a glimmer of hope on my darkest days. I found myself latching on to survival stories and they certainly gave my confidence a much-needed boost.

More and more, I see that out of suffering come the most compassionate and caring souls. Instead of wallowing in self-pity they choose to turn something negative into something positive by helping others face their own crisis. Today I never mind talking to someone who has been newly diagnosed with cancer. I do hope in some small way I help them to find their own healer within and maybe see their own light at the end of the tunnel when all seem dark and depressing. People talk daily about heroes being someone who have gained much media attention for achieving something amazing like climbing Mount Everest or sailing around the world. Yes! they are heroes, but I also believe that our world is full of silent heroes. I meet people everyday that live with daily worries, illnesses, and handicaps and yet still manage to get up and go, no matter how many times they fall. They have the power to keep smiling, overcoming numerous obstacles. Courage does take on many forms. It takes courage to live with pain be it emotional or physical. It takes courage to live with it without complaining and to still find laughter and joy in each new day. They walk the walk every day in their own quiet heroic way without anyone, even those close to them even realizing it. It is a constant source of inspiration to me to meet people like this and it is truly a privilege to get to know them.

My prayers were being answered in many ways and the peace of mind I so wished for was being nurtured and encouraged by people who came my way. Just when I felt I couldn't face another day, someone or something would come along and catch me at the time when I needed help most. One of these things was in the form of a book given to me as a present. It was called, *Getting Well Again* by Carol and Stephanie Simonton. Up to that point I had been trying to develop a positive mental attitude, believing that if I had peace of mind then my healing process would be easier. I was working purely on my own instincts, and had plenty of doubts about the benefit's, if any, that were to be gained from learning to relax and training my thoughts in a positive way. Down through the years I was trained to deal with physical illness/symptoms, so I never really delved too deeply into the emotional/psychological aspects of the disease. To be honest I was quite skeptical, so even though I was doing certain things, as I said earlier, I really was just going through the motions.

This book certainly gave me hope and a strong belief that I was on the right track. For the first time, I really did feel that I had some power and had the ability to take control. It was full of case studies about the psychological element of illness and how a person with cancer can help to create a healing environment through techniques such as mental imagery, meditation, and relaxation. It was the first of many such books I read and we should never underestimate the power of the written word. From that day I knew my mind was very strong and in my heart and soul I knew how I used it would

effect how I dealt with my illness and indeed even it's outcome. And so I started to practice what I was reading in the
book. I visualized and created positive mental images in my
mind. I created and image of a little animal going around my
veins, gobbling up anything that shouldn't be there. This image became almost constant no matter where I was or what
I was doing. Sometimes I even gave this little animal a torch
so he could see in the dark! When chemotherapy was being
given, instead of thinking of all the negative side effects, I
tried to look on it as a stream of crystal clear water flowing
through my veins, bringing healing wherever it went. Everyday I told myself I was getting stronger and healthy. You the
reader, at this stage may be starting to question my sanity,
but believe me these thoughts were better than those dark
negative ones that were always lurking in corners ready to
cause havoc to my way of thinking.

I had the luxury of experiencing massage for the very first
time as a result of my illness. We all affect each other by our
actions and words on our journey through life. As a nurse I
had cared for numerous people throughout my career. Some
years earlier I looked after a gentleman who was terminally
ill, and now in my hour of need his daughter Marian, came
along offering me the gift of regular massages throughout my
chemotherapy. At this stage I had become very good at accepting any help that came my way. So once I got the permission from my Oncologist, those massages became something
I looked forward to each week. Lying on the massage table
was an opportunity to let go and just be, which was a huge
form of healing. It seemed that everything I was doing or
having done for me, were building on each other, giving me
the tools I needed to find that inner strength that we all have
but don't always tap into. Marian was truly giving from the
heart when she offered me her gift. Her kindness inspired me

to train as a Massage Therapist myself, knowing how powerful a healing tool it can be in the midst of a crisis. Her simple act of kindness and help not only helped me but also inspired me to pass that help on to someone else through massage... and so the cycle of life continues.

Christmas was drawing near and instead of the usual fuss, I had no choice but to stand back and just let it happen. Usually I would be planning for weeks beforehand but I was so tired that year I had to take it easy. As a result of this, our Christmas was easier, calmer and more relaxed. One evening very close to Christmas day I found myself sitting in our local Church absorbing the atmosphere of silence, watching the candles flickering as they burned. I had been feeling particularly sad that day, and so I felt a great peace sitting there in the semi-darkness. Walking back through our busy streets to my home, the mad frenzy of Christmas shoppers was like a slap in the face. Normally I would have been in the midst of them all, but at that moment I felt like running back to the sanctuary of the Church to get away from the crowds of stressed and tense faces in front of me. Having to step back from it all was an eye-opener, and to this day I try to constantly remind myself not to get too caught up in the commercialism of it all at Christmas.

Mary, our daughter, had often asked about getting a dog and over the years we always found reasons not to as the time never seemed right. That Christmas she was more persistent, and I halfheartedly thought about getting one. As a child we always had a family pet as my father had a great love for animals. My memory of him and his loyal little terrier Judy, brings a smile to my face as I write, as they were inseparable and adored each other. He nursed her back to health on a few occasions and whenever he was away for any length of time she would pine for him until he came back. He died suddenly in 1979 and a few months after his death we found his beloved Judy dead at our back door. She had lost her friend and just pined away until she died. My memory of Judy was fresh in my mind as I thought about getting a dog that Christmas, so I decided that maybe the time was right.

As I said earlier about coincidences happening, it seemed that once I had decided to get a dog there was one ready and waiting for us! Sitting waiting to have my chemotherapy, I mentioned to a lady that we were thinking of getting a dog. Her sister who was with her, happened to work in a boarding kennels, and they were looking for a home for a Yorkshire terrier. So it was that easy, and with much excitement, Jessie came to live with us on Christmas Eve, sporting a big red bow on her head, bringing with her much needed joy and happiness to our house. I think my father had a part in it all, and knew exactly what we needed at that time to give us all a lift. I truly believe that animals bring so much love and happiness to a home and our home now has two dogs. Jessie being the boss, as she got here first, and Bonzo, a Jack Russell, who came to live with us in 2003. Both are loved dearly and bring out the best in us all as a family and are totally spoilt. A car hit Bonzo our second dog, when he was a pup and as a result he has a head injury that causes him to continuously go around in circles. So if any of us are having an "off" day he always manages to bring a smile to our faces. The love and attention we give to animals comes back to us ten times over and we have so much to learn from them. Their instincts and loyalty are very strong and throughout my chemotherapy Jessie would usually be found lying next to me especially on those "off" days. She would know when I was unwell and lying beside me was her way of showing it.

Christmas is a time when we reflect on the year gone by, wonder about what lies ahead. Every year, as I put the decorations back into their boxes, I would fleetingly think about what changes/events would happen before Christmas came around once more. As I packed the boxes that year, the reality of my uncertain future was more than fleeting. The possibility of not being around the following year was very real and definite, no matter how positive I was. The utter sadness of not being with my family was overwhelming so I decided to write letters to them all just in case...I hid them among the tinsel and baubles and I felt a certain comfort in having done it. Thankfully I remembered to find them the following year and happily burnt them in the fire. It seemed, that once I started writing I couldn't stop, so I wrote to my sisters, brothers, friends and practically everyone I could think of. It became rather complicated as I thought I'd forget someone, thus causing upset so luckily I was the only one to see them. I think it was just my way of expressing on paper what I found hard to say in words. Reading back over them some time later was embarrassing for me as they were very emotional and were of no benefit to anyone but myself at the time I wrote them. I did accept them as a much-needed release of what I needed to say at that time. I suppose that's why I found myself writing this book as I realized how beneficial healing process writing is for me. And it really is my own form of constant healing that I hope in this circle of life will get published and help someone else.

Coming to the end of my chemotherapy I seemed to be at an all time low, both mentally and physically. Without realizing it I had all of the classic symptoms of depression. Outwardly I appeared relatively normal. I was able to have a conversation about the most trivial of things; I could sit through lunch with a friend and act as though I was okay. In reality I was struggling to get through each hour. It seemed that I had developed two personalities. One for public show that seemed to be coping, while all the time I was slowly and painfully dying inside. As I allowed this to continue I found myself going deeper and deeper into this mood. It was getting harder and harder to see any light at the end of the tunnel. To get through a normal day became a huge effort and the pressure of trying to keep up the façade of being okay gradually took it's toll so thank God I told my Oncologist how I was feeling. The very act of saying it out loud was a huge relief and from then onwards I began to heal. He recommended a course of anti-depressants for a few months, which at first I was reluctant to take but luckily I had the sense to follow his advice. I can honestly say it was the best thing I could have done at that time. They were a much-needed crutch, and gave me back my self-control and strength to continue my healing journey. I knew I had to learn to live my life in a more relaxed, stress free way but making these life changes took effort and energy that I didn't have at that time. So the anti-depressants helped me through those few months allowing me to explore ways to relax and deal with stress. As soon as I felt in control again I gradually weaned myself off them, and thankfully I have never looked back. My attitude towards anti-depressants has changed though, and I feel that should the occasion arise again where I cannot cope and need some help, I would have no hesitation in taking them again. We should not see them as a sign of weakness or failure. There really is nothing at all wrong with admitting we need help to get us through a difficult time. Like many other medications they have their place.

And so February came and my chemotherapy was over. Instead of feeling elated as I thought I would be when I reached this milestone, I felt a whole barrage of mixed emotions. My three weekly visit's to the hospital had become a form of security, and now I was finished I knew I had to start getting back some semblance of normality. My head was full of a thousand thoughts. I didn't have to see my Oncologist for a month so I was totally on my own, or so I felt. It was one of the strangest days. On one hand it was great to have come so far but on the other hand I knew I had to face the real world and live my life as best I could, not wondering constantly if every ache or pain was the cancer back again. Knowing that chemotherapy drugs were being given every three weeks was a security blanket, now that was over I felt the real test was beginning, Would the cancer come back? Was it all gone? Once again I was running away with myself—wanting to be months ahead knowing that the longer I remained cancer free the better my chance of survival. Doing this was driving me insane, so I knew I had to do some serious talking to myself. I felt my fear had the ability to get out of hand if I didn't take control of it. I was afraid to plan any kind of future because of the possibility the cancer may come back.

Okay, I had survived chemotherapy. I was still here, but things would never be the same again. I knew I had tapped into an inner strength and wanted to continue on that journey so I started exploring what therapies etc., would help me to live my life in a new and more meaningful way. People suggested Arc House in Dublin as it offered support for people affected by cancer. Now Dublin isn't too far from Gorey but I was so sick of travelling to hospitals that I wanted something nearer home. I thought I'd see what our local Holistic Center had to offer. It certainly had a lot of therapies and classes going on. To someone like me who knew very little about the whole area of complimentary medicine it was a bit confusing to say the least. Already I knew I wanted to continue building on my own inner strength so rather than blindly signing up for different classes I took home their list to browse through at my leisure. There were so many therapies available promising all sorts. In fact I felt quite stressed wondering which ones I would try. Now I knew the last thing I needed was stress in my life so I made a decision to do absolutely nothing and to just enjoy the feeling of being well again.

People travel to wonder at the height of mountains, at the huge waves of the sea, at the long courses of the rivers, at the vast compass of the ocean, at the circular motion of the stars, and they pass by themselves, without wondering.

St. Augustine

Chapter Six

IF YOU ARE UNFORTUANTE ENOUGH to be told you have cancer, or indeed any serious illness where you come face to face with your mortality the future suddenly becomes very uncertain. This uncertainty creates a huge sense of urgency about life. All those "maybe someday" and "perhaps some-time" thoughts appear pointless. Instead, there is an over-whelming need to do things in the here and now. For most of us life is fairly routine and mundane with only minor hiccups along the way. A cancer diagnosis changes all that. Everything that was bothersome before suddenly appears so very insignificant. Faced with this scenario a whole new set of coping skills are needed.

I was, as anyone would be, unprepared for what I faced, and felt I had so much to learn so that I could live my life in a peaceful way that was as worry free as possible. Now that chemotherapy and all it's drama was over the real learning was only beginning. From my diagnosis and right through all my chemotherapy I was on a survival mission to get through it. Now I had to learn to live again. I felt that nothing would ever be the same but in this survival mode I was more than willing to accept change and a new way of living. Initially, I was quite content to just be, doing the daily things all mothers do. It was lovely to go about my daily routine in my own home. Looking back on that time I believe I was taking back some sense of control, I was like an animal marking it's territory. The nurturing instinct was very strong and I got a great sense of comfort and satisfaction from cooking meals and baking for my family. The very basic task of something as simple as baking brown bread can be so very rewarding. The preparation, cooking and subsequent pleasure of seeing it being enjoyed with relish is such a source of basic satisfaction and fulfilment. Even though I had been planning all sorts of holidays in my head I was quite happy to just be at home in my own place. It's what I needed at that time to put me back on an even footing in my life.

My hair was growing slowly and as soon as it was long enough I was off to the hairdressers getting my blonde highlights once more. Being blonde again gave me back a certain confidence, a feeling of normality. I met someone shortly after being to the hairdressers and she said, "it's great to see you're back to yourself again." She didn't comment on my highlights but the colour did bring me back to myself in a strange way. She was so right, it was as if I was someone else for a while and being blonde again had given me back my identity. I do know that self-confidence has as much to do with our inner as well as our outer selves but it certainly doesn't do us any harm to feel that we are looking good. I had gained quite a lot of weight throughout my treatment; it wasn't something I liked very much, always refusing to look at the scales when I was weighed at my check ups! The extra weight seems to be part of the new me and my attitude now is to eat sensibly and take lots of exercise, all which helps me to feel good about myself. Taking Tamoxofin medication (an oestrogen inhibitor) seems to contribute to my weight gain so I'm looking forward to completing the five-year recommended course and getting my body back.

My first check up came around and I felt a sense of achievement to have come so far. Before a catastrophe, we can't imagine how we will cope and I always thought cancer was my worst nightmare. I had survived though, it had happened to me and I was suddenly finding strength in me that I never knew I had. The reality of course is that all of us have the ability to do so much more than we think we are capable of. Sitting in front of Seamus O'Reilly, my oncologist that day, I wanted him to be able to tell me I was cured and that the cancer was never going to come back. Of course he couldn't do that, no one had the ability to tell me I was never going to get sick again. Even without a cancer diagnosis no one can predict how healthy we will be or how long we are going to live. Our lifestyle will help give some idea of our risk of disease but that's all it will do. Seamus could tell me that all was well that day as I sat in front of him. I was anxious for reassurance so I could put it all behind me and say that it was over and finished with. I wanted him to organise scans for every part of me, but being realistic what would that prove; all clear that day, what about next week, next year, and so on. I knew I couldn't keep depending on tests/scans, etc. for constant reassurance and I certainly didn't want to live my life going from one hospital department to another. Life just would not be worth living and I wanted to live.

My next appointment was arranged for three months later, which seemed like an eternity and yet another part of me thought, "well, he must think I'm going to live until then." No matter how positive I was trying to be those dark thoughts were never far away. Eventually I learned to accept them as part of me and this acceptance took away some of their control. In a funny way, having surgery/chemotherapy etc is the easy part. Learning to live, and I mean living relatively worry free between doctor's visit's is the hard bit. I didn't want to spend my time counting the days until my next check up. Waiting for the results of yet another scan to give me permission and reassurance to exist for another day, to me that's not living but existing. Okay, it is essential and reassuring to have our routine check-ups and tests but being totally honest I was sick of hospitals and all that went with them, no matter how much I knew they had contributed to my health.

Knowing I wasn't going to see my oncologist for three whole months was like being sent back to the reality of the big bad world. The regular hospital visit's were over and took with them my security blanket because if ever I had a worry or query I knew my next visit was never too far away. The time had come to see once more what our local holistic centre had to offer me. I knew the time was right for some extra help. I needed to learn to live my life in a new way. I wanted to put the cancer behind me but it had happened, I couldn't deny it. I needed to learn from it. Okay, we all have to die but let it be on our own terms and in our own good time. I never asked my oncologist what he thought my prognosis would be. I did know that I had a very big aggressive lump and I had asked lots of questions about it. I suppose fear held me back from letting someone estimate how long my life was going to be. After all a doctor's prognosis is hypothetical, he can try based on other people's experience give you a prognosis, but at the end of the day I wanted to stay in control of my illness until I was drawing my last breath. I didn't want anyone, no matter how brilliant they were telling me I had two, five, possibly ten years to live. I knew I had an uncertain future but I was also learning the importance of today and of living in the present and when it came right down to it that's all anyone has...cancer diagnosis or not.

My illness was not a failure but a challenge, presenting me with the chance to learn my body's needs. If we cut our hand-our natural healing mechanism deals automatically with the healing, it sees that the food we eat is properly distributed throughout our body helping to maintain our health. When you think about it our bodies are truly wonderful and amazing, constantly working and continuously renewing, changing and healing. I needed to develop my mind in a way that it could focus on constantly instructing my own repair/healing mechanism in the right way. So instead of consciously creating negative thoughts of disease I could be consciously creating health.

Doctors and medical staff sometimes say, "such a limb/ organ is useless or non functioning." By doing this, they are telling our intrinsic healing mechanism that there is no hope. Hopelessness is such a terrible word. It can distort our minds at a time when we should be directing each thought constructively until we hold only thoughts that contain the power to build up and heal. It is so important to have hope, and in the face of serious illness to remember you are still alive, you are only as helpless as you think you are- or want to be, healing can and does happen. Now don't get me wrong I'm not for one minute saying that I'm giving false, unrealistic hope; I'm saying how good a feeling it is to be in charge and feel somewhat in control. The feeling of self-empowerment is the right of all living beings. Illness shouldn't mean that we immediately become passive and accepting of all that is done to us. No matter what our condition is we can still all have realistic goals and hopes to work towards no matter how small and insignificant they seem to anyone else.

Awakening to the fact that I had some control over my own destiny was a great sense of relief tinged with a great sense of responsibility. Anything that would help me was essential. Nobody learns from life by being told what to do. The only way I knew I would learn was by experimenting. Finding what would and wouldn't work and then choosing what I felt was right for me to enhance my healing process. We really do become free when we realise that we need many lessons to help bring us closer to knowing and accepting ourselves. Healing is the restorative ability available to everyone, it sometimes needs to be assisted or facilitated by another person or sometimes it will manifest it'self. Everyone has his or her own intrinsic healing process and everyone's own process is unique and individual. I had gratefully accepted surgery/chemotherapy as the scientific proven healing and it had worked. I knew that I had in some small way, tapped into my own healing through what I had been doing, i.e. creating positive mental images, listening to music, massage and writing my thoughts on paper. All seemed to be helping me to touch some deep part of myself where I instinctively knew my real strength lay.

I was more than willing to continue searching so I enrolled in a yoga class at the holistic centre. Between the beautifully relaxing room at the centre and the calmness and serenity of Sadie, our yoga instructor, it was impossible not to relax. The philosophy of deep breathing exercises, gentle stretches, candle gazing and meditation soon had me hooked and it was enough to have a room full of people gone way beyond mere relaxation. So often at the end of a class the only sounds would be a few gentle snores coming from different corners of the room. Each thing acted as a building block coming together, helping me to be more relaxed and at peace with myself. When someone decides to run a marathon they have to do more than just make the decision, they have to dedicate themselves to a strict training regime allowing them to complete the task. Couldn't the same be said about deciding to be positive? The decision just isn't enough, like our physical body, our minds need training and looking after as well and I was a more than willing student. All this relaxation was not only benefiting me but those around me as well, especially my immediate family as I think I was easier to live with...most of the time anyway!

Going to the holistic centre for the weekly yoga classes was a great way for me to be up to date with what else was happening there. So, as if I was sampling the menu in a restaurant I did the same with their lists of therapies/classes, etc., discovering what I did and didn't like. It seemed that something in me had woken up and I was discovering a whole new world of wonderful people that I had never really noticed before. I have to say here that I often drove past the holistic centre before I got sick without giving it a second thought, but then I suppose I wasn't searching so my mind was probably closed to what was on offer there. As I said before, being a nurse I was more focussed on the science behind everything and really the word "holistic" didn't come into play. The "science," concentrating on treating the illness, whereas holistic means treating the whole person and maintaining health. The idea of maintaining health/wellness is based on the knowledge that we are complex beings. From moment to moment there is a continuous subtle interaction between mind body and spirit, with all of them connecting to the environment in which we live and with other beings that inhabit it.

Once I started all this exploring it seemed so easy. One thing seemed to lead to another. Before I got sick my mind was certainly closed to words like auras, energy fields, self-healing etc. Rex Dunlop a kinesiologist, had just joined the centre and he had started meditation workshops which sounded interesting so I joined up. Between yoga on a Monday night, mediation on a Friday night, I was certainly well on my way to finding my inner calm! On top of that I was reading countless books on mind/body/spirit topics, so I wouldn't be exaggerating if I said that for a while I was floating up high somewhere in the clouds, not a bad place to be I might add, in fact quite a good feeling but we all have to live in the real world as well. I could question here what is real, our physical/scientific world or our spiritual one. Along the way I've decided that they are all real but the real test is not to constantly float along in the clouds but to remain grounded as well and walk firmly and responsibly on the earth.

Before I reached that conclusion though I drove everyone around me insane telling them all about the things I was doing and what they should be doing as well to find themselves. There really is nothing as bad as a born again... whatever! Luckily my family and friends tolerated me and allowed me to ramble on and on. I'm sure they were often thinking, "here she goes again"! I suddenly renewed a teenage interest I had with the smell of incense, so it was frequently used in our house. Our sons Niall and Eoin, would put their eyes up to heaven when they would come in from school being greeted by the sometimes-overpowering smells floating around the house! I have no doubt they were all secretly questioning my sanity. This was proven to me one day when Michael was dropping me off at the centre. Mary our daughter, remarked to no one in particular, "Oh! she's off to one of 'those' classes with all 'those' new friends"! I think they had an image of a group of people in long flowing dresses levitating two feet off the ground in a constant state of self obsessed bliss! There's no doubt about it though I was definitely going through a time of change within myself. It was a deeply personal experience and it seemed that I had truly tapped into my soul the thinker of my thoughts. Now before you start thinking that I have turned into a Saint Bernadette the positive, be assured I am a long way from canonisation. I'm still me warts and all, but the "me" is a happier, more peaceful person. I'm happy being alone with my thoughts and to be able to do that is a gift. I feel fulfilled and privileged to be able to love and appreciate life so much. To be able to let go of a lot of what I thought was necessary and important. I also know that as much as I love to talk I need silence as well to be truly alone with myself so that I can maintain that peace. I realised too that it was my journey. There was no need for me to shout it from the rooftops or to expect everyone around me to feel what I was feeling and suddenly do what I was doing because I thought it was right. My journey was and is not theirs. We all find our own way and have our own unique journey to discover. It was enough then for me to stop trying to change everyone around me and accept the love and support of Michael, our children ,family and friends.

I had my first mammogram since my surgery and it was another milestone on my path. I faced it with a certain dread not only because of the possible results, but also because I absolutely hated the procedure. Having one's breast flattened and squashed is far from pleasant, even if it is only for a short time. I'd certainly be willing to bet that it had to be a man who invented that machine! I remarked to the lady carrying out the procedure how much I hated having it done. Her reply was "aren't you lucky then you only have one"! She meant well, I'm sure, but I don't think she really realised what she had said. "Lucky" not quite being the word I would have used...results were clear which was a relief as it is hard not to let worry come to the surface when you are waiting for that phone call. I have decided that too many hospital tests are totally counterproductive. Now don't get me wrong here. Of course they are essential. The thing is I didn't want to become too dependent on them. I didn't want to be on a roller coaster of going from one appointment to another being scanned and x rayed. I certainly didn't want to run to my doctor with every ache and pain. It would seem then as if my life was permanently on hold as I waited for results of yet another test. I try and stay away from hospitals as much as possible. I'm not saying that I would be so foolish as to ignore anything unusual as I do find my regular check ups reassuring and thankfully all remains well.

And so decision time had come, should or shouldn't I go back nursing. After a cancer diagnosis people often say how good it is to get past two years, five years and so on. They are right of course and I certainly didn't want to sit around counting the months and years waiting for those significant milestones to pass. On the other hand, I wasn't at all ready to face being back working as a community nurse. It just didn't feel right for me and at that time I couldn't imagine myself working in a situation where there was always so much to do and never enough hours in the day. Luckily I didn't have a permanent job so I wasn't faced with the decision of leaving a permanent secure position. I wasn't losing any regular financial security by deciding to take time out, as my job had been mainly part time. I decided then it was as good a time as any to press the reset button on my life and try something else. I also knew how lucky I was to have Michael's unending support in whatever decision I made. His support is quiet, consistent and unending and I do know and appreciate how lucky I am to have that. Not everyone is given the opportunity to explore other areas in their life, as often work and family commitments just don't allow it. Mind you he reminds me that he's expecting millions from all the time I've spent writing this book!...if it ever get's published that is.

The regular massages from Marian had a big impact on me. The feeling of peace that I experienced from it was fresh in my mind and so I gave serious consideration to training as a therapist myself. The idea of returning to study was quite daunting but I made a few enquiries anyway. I knew I wanted to learn more than just anatomy and physiology and the physical element of massage. I saw an advertisement in one of the Sunday papers for a course at The Healing House in Dublin. It offered a combination of physical massage, anatomy and physiology and most importantly to me the subtle levels of healing and understanding of the spiritual journey. Following a phone call to Brenda McKenna, the course coordinator, I decided to enrol and so was all set to start in September. The course was to run from September 2001 to June 2002. A part of me couldn't believe that I was going back to study again but it felt right and I was learning to go with my gut feeling more and more. It was scary though; After all I was a 42-year-old one breasted woman tormented by hot flushes and mood swings putting myself into a totally unknown situation. There were loads of reasons as to why I shouldn't do it but somebody somewhere was telling me that it was a good decision. So with my mind made up the summer slipped by with a mixture of sad and happy days. The sadness being like a form of mourning for the old me, an acknowledgment and acceptance of letting go of old ways and habit's. I would acknowledge and give myself permission to be sad and it would pass bringing happiness in the anticipation of new beginnings and appreciation of a bright future.

The present moment is never unbearable if you live in it fully. What is unbearable is to have your body here at 10 a.m. and your mind at 6 p.m., your body in Bombay and your mind in San Francisco!

Anthony de Mello

Chapter Seven

As I struggled through my first homework assignment for the massage course I seriously questioned what I had let myself in for. Pages and pages of anatomy and physiology questions stared up at me giving my poor brain cells a major shock. It was twenty years or so since I had qualified as a nurse, so it was quite difficult to start studying once more. After I had completed the first assignment, which took many hours of drawing diagrams and writing, I was mentally exhausted not to mention having a very stiff neck from all the writing! I was using muscles and brain cells that hadn't been used in years! Mind you, once I got over that first shock I rather enjoyed learning again.

I always felt a great sense of achievement when I completed a homework assignment. I was able to lose myself for hours on end, drawing diagrams and writing about the workings of the human body. Unknown to myself, the cancer was no longer the constant thought in my head. Okay, I was a woman with a mastectomy and the scar was a constant reminder but it was in my past. Being in a whole new situation with a whole new group of people was the best thing I could have done as it lessened the potency of the cancer for me.

That's not to say that I found it easy. The practical side of the course involved learning the actual massage techniques. This meant being paired in twos, practising massage strokes on each other under the ever-watchful eye of our tutor, Brenda McKenna. I obviously hadn't given this too much thought beforehand because if I had I probably wouldn't have even started the course. The reality of learning our technique on each other meant getting undressed in a room full of fellow classmates that really were strangers to me. We then took turns lying on the massage tables while we learned the basic art of massage. The first few times were difficult for me, as I felt very exposed, embarrassed and vulnerable. I gradually got used to it and I can now say it really helped me get over any hang-ups I had about my body; it's far from perfect shape, it's stretch marks from having three children and the latest addition—the mastectomy scar. Accepting my body with all it's flaws meant I could then relax and enjoy the whole experience of the massage experience.

Ironically, my exams fell on the date exactly two years since I had found my breast lump and it was a great sense of achievement to complete the exam and go on to receive my diploma. Cancer intensifies all these moments and continues to do so. There is always a strong sense of awareness in reaching a new stage in life or completing something. I'm not saying that I have achieved great and wonderful things. We are not all cut out to make amazing changes in our lives but having faced our own mortality we realise those small stepping-stones in our lives become great achievements for us. Following a check up I always feel a great sense of gratitude and wonderment when I'm told that all is well. I'd say to myself "imagine that, my body hasn't let me down after all," —now that to me is a very important milestone. Michael and I went to Prague for a long weekend and when we arrived in the very beautiful snow-covered city I felt so lucky to be there it was another stepping stone for me. You see, I had spent many dark "chemo" days planning trips and wondering if I would ever go anywhere. It was as though I was recapturing the very essence of a childhood reality and so I was seeing and experiencing everything as if for the very first time. Cancer does teach us to notice things, what we should and shouldn't care about, and so leaves us feeling more fulfilled and privileged to be alive. To others our milestones may seem small but to us they are big steps. I got through the whole cancer experience and didn't "crack up" as I thought I would; now that's an achievement. The fact that Michael and I have three great children is without doubt one of our greatest achievements of all. Of course it has to be said, that as a family we managed to get through all the bad days without actually killing each other is another miracle that has to be acknowledged.

I do sometimes feel a great sense of urgency about life as if there is so much to do and never enough time. As I write this, we are in the process of planning a new kitchen, something I'm really looking forward to. That sense of urgency about time is there, as I want to be able to enjoy it **now**. You see, the anticipation of a looking forward to a future event is often tinged with a little fear as a result of having had cancer. I accept the reality of that fear as part of me and it by no means is the controlling influence in my life. Apart from the practicalities of home improvements and rearing our family, there are so many little things I want to do. I want to dive into the sea without any fear, learn to play the piano, ride the biggest roller-coaster and not go insane with panic and, oh yeah, I want to get a book published and maybe even two. If you are reading this, well then I've achieved some of my dreams!!

I live with the reality of cancer but it's intensity becomes less and less as time passes. When I hear about someone who has died of breast cancer I go through a whole range of emotions. In the early stages these emotions were all consuming and terrifying and were so intense I'd feel like giving up there and then. But when you have a cancer diagnosis you can't afford the luxury of doing that, we have to work that bit harder not to give in to self-pity and negative thinking. Okay, it's important to acknowledge these fears and emotions, deal with them as best we know how and then move on. Now, when I hear about someone who has died the emotion is still there but not quite as intense. I have learned so much over the past few years and that learning has given me the strength and wisdom to be able to live with my..."self" in a happy contented way. Everyone's journey is unique and personal to them, and it is theirs alone, not mine. We are all individuals on our own path and although we are affected by other people's good and bad stories, the reality is we are all on our own journey. They are not us and we are not them no matter how we identify with their story. We must learn to accept the mystery of this weird and wonderful thing called life. I do question sometimes why I'm still here, when others haven't been so lucky, but there are no clear answers, just lots and lots of maybes. Life has to be learned and I do know it cannot always be explained. It reveals it's own mysteries continuously, moulding and shaping our personality as we go along so we are able to deal with the good and bad that comes our way.

Cancer diagnosis or not, we should leave the past in the

past where it belongs, the future in the future and so just live in the moment where we are at any given time. The more we consciously put this into practice, the easier it becomes. As I become more in tune with my body's needs, I no longer push it to it's limit's; instead I consciously try to treat it with respect. I was inclined to beat myself up about how I constantly pushed myself before I got sick. "If I knew then what I know now" springs to mind. For a while I was inclined to blame myself for contributing to my illness, but I have learned to accept myself as I was then and be thankful and appreciative of all I have learned since then. So the past is gone and with that conscious realisation there comes a freedom and peace in the knowledge that everything passes and nothing stays the same and in letting go there is a self forgiveness so we are able to cherish the here and now and be at peace

When our eldest son, Eoin, went to college in September 2003 we were delighted that he had achieved what he wanted. Nothing prepared me for the overwhelming emotions I felt when he left home for the first time. Now don't get me wrong, I was delighted to see him become independent and I certainly wouldn't have wanted him at home under my feet. The floodgates opened inside me, and once the tears started I just lost all control of them. Michael constantly reassured me that he would be okay, and of course I knew he would be, but it wasn't about that at all. I knew in my mind it was related to the cancer, to what might have been, to the reality that I might not have been there at that stepping stone in his life. Also, it was a reminder once again of my uncertain future and so I was off again, running away with myself, wondering a million "what if's." No matter how hard we work at being positive and learning to live in the present, we still run away with ourselves from time to time. The thing is though, through all the learning and soul searching we become more and more fine-tuned to our inner selves and so we are more attentive to our needs and complex emotions. Our awareness means that we can never deny or run away from our emotions again. We may try but they will challenge us again and again. Once we learn then to trust the wisdom of our soul, we will always have our inner guide directing us. It is, however, a constant discipline that takes daily revising and reminding.

I knew I needed to deal with whatever was going on as I didn't want to fall into the black hole of depression again. Taking anti-depressants didn't appeal to me without first giving some other alternative a try. They had helped me when I was coming to the end of my treatment and were what I needed at that time when I hadn't the physical energy to explore other options. I was now much stronger in every way and more confident that I had the ability to deal with whatever was happening. I decided to try counselling to see where it would lead. So, before I got cold feet I made an appointment to see Freda Hanley, a psychotherapist, providing free counselling for anyone affected by cancer. This service came about as a result of fund-raising by a local lady, who through her own experience with breast cancer saw the need for such a service in the area. As I said before, out of someone's own trauma can come so much positive things and this service being provided free was one such positive thing, as Freda has and still does help so many people.

Never having had counselling before I didn't know what to expect. Basically, I thought I'll do all the talking, [which wasn't a problem for me], and Freda would sit quietly and listen. I realised very early on that even though I could talk the hind legs off a donkey, I wasn't too comfortable talking constantly about myself and my own needs. I felt rather "self"…indulgent sitting there giving myself loads of attention. Over time though I could see that it was helping me so I got over the guilt thing pretty fast! The old expression "getting it all off your chest" really does have a literal meaning and although it was exhausting to sit constantly talking about myself it was wonderful to clear out the mental clutter in the attic of my mind. All this talking helped me to see things clearly and understand myself more. If we don't clear out all this clutter from time to time, we become "all mixed up" and we can't see the wood for the trees! I think counselling/psychotherapy has, in some way, replaced the cathartic tradition of going to confession in our lives. Isn't it almost the same, going into a room and getting all the bad stuff off your chest? Mind you my mother's tradition of making us go to confession every First Friday was a pointless exercise for me as I usually spent my time making up a list of so called sins so I'd have something to say to the priest. Things like…I cursed twice…I said bad things about my friend three times. I'm sure the poor priest must have been smiling to himself.

So I have to say I managed to get used to Eoin being away from home. Now don't get me wrong I love him and all my children so very much…but less cooking…cleaning… ironing isn't so bad once in a while. I like to think that the best we can give our children are roots to ground them and wings to fly.

Come to the edge, he said. They said, we are afraid. Come to the edge, he said. They came. He pushed them and they flew.

Guillaume Apollinaire

Chapter Eight

So HAS MY LIFE CHANGED, have I changed? Yes, I believe it has and I have too. Do I want to roll back the clock and delete the whole cancer experience? Do you know what, I don't think so.

To answer the first question more thoroughly, I'm still living in the same house with the same husband and children, doing the same daily mundane tasks of cooking, cleaning, ironing, washing, school runs, etc., etc. I still tolerate hot flushes, mood swings, mine as well as those of our teenagers! Because of my hot flushes my poor family are permanently frozen, as I cannot tolerate too much heat in the house. They are driven mad with fans whirling and windows open, but sure they tolerate me, most of the time anyway...I still have many, many questions about life and all the many ups and downs that go with it.

I can see and realise though that everything in my life, no matter how mundane, is significant enough to be a continuous source of learning and inspiration for me. All my soul searching has helped me to find amazing resources inside myself, resources; I might add that we all have. To find these I had to go through the bad bit's and so be able to let go and move on. Who we really are has nothing to do with material wealth or success, but it has everything to do with how we view ourselves inside. This knowledge involves trusting the unknown, living in the here and now and surrendering to whatever each new day brings. All the diets and exercises in the world will not counterbalance the effect of emotional pain. I firmly believe that our emotions do affect our body in both good and bad ways. Our thoughts are real no matter how much we try to deny them. They will always be there, with their own energy that can create healing and peace or pain and anguish. Ask yourself this question, when you are upset, angry, afraid, where do you feel it in your body? The expressions we use daily without thought will answer the question in a very simple way. I have a lump in my throat, a broken heart, butterflies in my tummy, the weight of the world on my shoulders. Haven't we all experienced these and isn't it safe to say they are coming from an emotional place? The real problem begins if they are not dealt with, that's when they start to create actual physical ailments.

When I started out on my cancer journey, all I asked for and craved was a peaceful mind. My need for this took me on a journey that began and ended with myself. I went through many highs and lows; I even went a bit daft for a while! I do like to believe that I have come through as a grounded person with realistic expectations about my life. I no longer drive my friends and family insane with talks of latest therapies, etc. I no longer run from one healing workshop to another. I try and live by what I have learned over the past few years. I still search for and love to read inspiring books (like this one!) because we never ever stop learning. I started out as a sceptic, but I now honestly believe in the role of a peaceful mind as part of our survival in life. Working as a Massage Therapist is a privilege. It is a source of constant healing for me to be able to work with people on a one to one basis and to be able to see what happens on many different levels when people accept responsibility for themselves. You see, health is not a permanent condition, but has to be revisited every day in our thoughts.

And to answer the second question more thoroughly, do I want to roll back the clock? The answer has to be no. Okay, I live with the knowledge that the cancer may come back at any time. But you see, the cancer has given me an opportunity to learn so much, to appreciate and accept the good and the bad. To appreciate and know that people will come and go, places and things will come and go. To be aware that by having good health and a peaceful mind, no matter how miserable the weather is, no matter how bad the traffic is, no matter how messy my house is, I can stop for a while… look to the sky and say "Yes, I'm alive."…And so, I am able to find a million tiny reasons each day, along with all my fears and worries, to smile and be at peace. And thankfully I cannot only smile but laugh as well.

So are you ever drawn to question your relevance in the world? Are you facing serious illness and asking yourself— why me? Are you disillusioned in your continued search for satisfaction from material wealth? Do you ever think, "is this all there is?" Well, if you are asking yourself questions you are already on your own search. Be gentle in that search, it cannot be forced. Listen to your own needs and be healed in the greatest way possible. Learn to trust life. The knowledge you have gained in your past will give you strength you need to deal with the future and so will sweeten the uncertainty about tomorrow. Learn that everything passes and nothing stays the same. Above all, allow yourself to be happy no matter what. We were born into this world to love life, have fun, to laugh and to cry. When your feet get tired on your long journey, don't be afraid to allow the hopes wishes and dreams of that future continue in your mind. You see, we all like to dream and if we only allow ourselves to do so when we are asleep we are denying ourselves endless possibilities of health, happiness and fun. And I for one am the ultimate dreamer!

Thank you for stepping into my shoes and walking with me for a while. I have tried to be as open and honest as possible. By doing this I hope you realise that it is okay to cry, to acknowledge and feel your pain. To touch the very centre of your own sorrow so that when you smile it will be from the heart, and when you are alone you will truly like your own company and be able to sit with yourself and be at peace. May your journey be a safe one full of peace and gentle healing.

Part Two

God grant me the serenity to accept the things I cannot change, courage to change the things I can, and wisdom to know the difference.

Prayer...My Way!

MY MOTHER CONSTANTLY PRAYED FOR US ALL. Novenas, rosaries, mass, and confessions were a big part of our family life. As a child I just accepted it as being "us," never really giving it too much thought. Sometimes I'd hope she would forget to say the nightly rosary but she never did. In fact she never missed an opportunity, so often when travelling in the car she would take out the rosary beads and off she'd go again. I'd ramble off the Hail Mary's, as fast as I could, usually thinking about something else to help the time go faster. I remember well when the rosary would start at home. My mother would kneel with her back to the television, thinking it was turned off. In actual fact we would have just turned down the sound so we could still see the picture. This, however, often caused it's own problems, as I'd be so busy trying to follow a television programme with no sound that I would forget how many Hail Mary's I'd have said! As a child growing up, and into my teenage years, it didn't mean an awful lot to me and I often felt that I was praying to a blank wall. The concept of God was hard to understand and just didn't seem real to me.

I went to Mass and all the Church ceremonies because I felt a sense of duty to go. Even though I still went and didn't like to miss it, I have to be honest and say I often daydreamed my way through the Sunday Mass. I would say that sense of duty was the reason behind my faith right up into my adult years. My mother's faith never wavered, and we always knew that she would pray even harder especially when we had any major event going on in our lives. She always instilled the belief that our sister Mary, who had died aged seventeen, was constantly looking after us and she reminded us to pray to her whenever we needed help. She would tell us that Mary was an angel in heaven always guiding and caring for us all. Her Lourdes medal, which she wore up to when she died, was given to each of us at important and significant times in our lives like exams, having our children or indeed any occasion that was deemed necessary. This seemed more realistic to me as I could picture her in my mind and so it was easier to ask her for help. She was like my contact to God and all the saints in heaven that my mother talked about.

When I was diagnosed with breast cancer, numerous people came to me with relics and prayers. I didn't have the energy to concentrate on all these prayers and for a while I wore myself out saying them all. I felt that if I didn't do all the novena's, go to all the Masses and generally become more devout, well then I wasn't going to get well. I prayed like mad, but once again, as in childhood, I was rambling off prayer after prayer. All the time putting myself under more pressure as I was trying too hard to force some sense of being heard by whatever or whoever was listening in the spiritual world. I was so busy with all my prayer leaflets that I didn't have time to think and I'd say God got weary of my voice day after day. I certainly wasn't achieving much of the peace of mind that I craved so much.

Eventually I got sense and realised that I was achieving nothing, so I stopped pushing myself and started to accept and acknowledge that there were so many people praying for me. This brought with it a great sense of peace and it was a constant source of positive energy at a time when I needed to be carried. I will never underestimate the power of receiving a thoughtful card or knowing that a candle has been lit in my name. Now, I sincerely believe these positive thoughts sent to someone are the most powerful prayers of all. So if ever I feel helpless in the face of someone else's troubles, not knowing what I can do to help, I simply think of them in a positive way asking God to send them healing and peace. By not trying too hard, and allowing myself to be carried in the knowledge that others were praying for me, gave me space to just stop and think. By accepting that I needed someone else to do all the praying was like a release, a handing over of all my troubles to someone else. It was as though I said, "I just can't deal with this, so I'll let myself be helped by all the prayers and thoughts that were coming my way." This conscious handing over allowed me to think clearly and in my own simple way I prayed...in the way that I found most meaningful as a child...to my sister and also my mother and father. It was a good place to start, as they were real to me. So I'd talk to them asking for help, for peace and anything else I could think of that would make my journey easier.

Everyone has his or her own way and everyone's own spiritual experience is unique, personal and individual. My belief is that it doesn't have to be at all complicated. It's much better to keep it really simple. When we try too hard or try to force it, we lose sight of who or what we are and ultimately to pray and understand God starts with understanding ourselves. Once we begin to see this we are then on our own journey of self-discovery. This journey will lead us to ask lots of questions about our role in the universe. If we have an open attitude we will learn so much from these questions. We will realise that it's okay to love ourselves, warts and all. We will stop trying too hard and realise that it is okay to just "be." By just "being" we become more in touch with our soul, which will be our guide. All this learning and awareness will make us realise that we are a very small part of something that is so much bigger. And with this realisation our need to constantly control will diminish leaving us with a sense of freedom and peace.

My search for peace took me to different places but ultimately that search became one of self-discovery. The very essence of my journey was and is based on silence because it is only by allowing ourselves to be still that we realise we have all the questions and answers needed for our journey. Through the art of learning to meditate I was able to allow the cobwebs to clear and so become awakened to trusting my own soul. In this awakening my awareness to all things become more defined and it was as though I was seeing and hearing for the very first time. I find the greatest peace among the silence of hills and fields and the sounds and beauty of nature. I truly believe that nature is our greatest teacher as it gently eases and relieves our troubled minds. Remind yourself of that wonderful feeling you get when standing in a place of beauty. As your awareness grows you feel a connection with all that is around you and so you feel at one with the healing energy of the earth.

Unfortunately, we don't spend enough time in nature so our connection to it has become diminished in our mad crazy and noisy world where we can't even hear ourselves. I believe this disconnection is leading to a feeling of loss, leaving us looking for something missing but not knowing what it is. No amount of wealth can fill this deep need within us. People are searching and will pay any amount of money to achieve peace of mind. If only they would stop and go right back to basics they would see they have all the answers within themselves. I looked after a wonderful gentleman some years ago who spent his whole life working as a farmer. His wife told me how he was often amused to hear about people going all over the world trying to "find themselves." He "found" himself every time he walked the fields, his daily chores on the land kept him connected to that sense of tranquillity and the healing power of the earth.

I believe the greatest gift we have is the ability to be alone with ourselves and be at peace in that solitude. In that peace I found myself once more and so felt a wonderful sense of homecoming. I really have come full circle; I go to Mass now, not because I have to but because I want to. Missing it doesn't leave me with a sense of guilt. I always feel a sense of peace for having been, and that's not to say that I don't still daydream at times!

As I said before I am certainly not a saint. I believe my day-to-day life is a prayer. My morning offering is a handing over of the day ahead to God, trusting that I will be guided in a way that is right for me. My nightime prayer is a thank you for the day and it's many gifts. My prayers are constantly being answered, not always in the way I would have asked but daily I feel blessed for all the little miracles that happen in my life. I believe my mother's prayers continue to work for me. What I found pointless growing up is now a source of comfort and peace for me. There is a wonderful sense of security to be gained from the ritual and discipline of Church ceremonies, so you could say that for me nothing has really changed. What I grew up with was there in me; I just had to find it myself, thus helping me to relearn it all over again in a way that had meaning for me. My mother's prayer book sit's beside my bed and I now find myself saying the prayers and novena's that she had accumulated over the years. I learned to meditate and I can now say that the ritual of saying prayers is probably the greatest meditation of all. It just took me a while to realise it. Saying prayers is wonderful when I just can't find my own words to say what I want or feel. For my mother's love and caring of me throughout her life I give thanks, and her death by no means stops my love for her. Even though I can't see her, I know in my heart and soul she is near me at all times.

We should never underestimate the power of our thoughts. Prayer thoughts sent out in a loving way have a wonderful effect on those who send them. All the good actions and thoughts we send to others are like a boomerang returning to benefit ourselves. So the expression "it is in giving that we receive" is so right. Of course, by thinking and dwelling on negative thoughts we will also attract and encourage similar ones back to us. So everything we do and say does affect others and will come back to us in a negative or positive way. We must constantly train our minds to cultivate positive thoughts of faith, well being and harmony. Once we become open to our thoughts we can never deny or run away from them ever again. They can travel deeply inwards bringing with them great happiness or great sadness and torment. Once we recognise and acknowledge whatever the thought is, it will cease to have control over us. By accepting the good and bad and not running away from them, we are taking control.

We all have a responsibility to ourselves, no matter how difficult life is, to ensure that each step we take through life is a good and positive one, each act we perform is one of goodness and from the heart. We need to remind ourselves every day that heaven is not off somewhere else but in our hearts and minds and most importantly we are only human and far from being perfect so it doesn't matter if we don't always get it right. The fact that we try is what matters and the trying and learning goes on and on. It is so important to remain grounded and keep a sense of balance as well as being spiritually aware. It's all very well to sit looking at the clouds, getting carried away with the beauty of it all, or sit in a Church all day praying when the rest of our lives are falling apart. We have to take responsibility for our lives as well as acknowledging our spirituality. In a way it is easier to focus on the spiritual aspect of life and float away on a cloud of "inner peace." By doing this we are denying the reality of our daily life and all it's problems and necessary routine that can seem totally mundane and boring. The real test is to combine all parts of our lives as best we know how and so, in amongst the daily humdrum of household chores, teenage tantrums and endless ironing we find those little moments that make it all worthwhile. You see how we carry out all these daily chores are a prayer in themselves.

Personally speaking there are times when I'd love to sail off into the sunset and become a born again sixties hippie with flowers in my hair and long flowing dresses thinking nothing only happy thoughts…but I suppose I better wait awhile!

Quietly in your own heart, say that you do not want to be afraid.

Deepak Chopra

The Healing Power of Touch

WE ALL LOVE TO BE LOVED. We experience that love for the first time from our mothers when, as newborn babies, we come into the world. That love is unconditional, everlasting and unchanging no matter what happens. A mother's basic instinct is to nurture, hug and embrace her child—so easing their distress and pain. To newborn babies that touch is contact and reassurance that they are being cared for and are safe. They learn very quickly to register the intent that goes with the touch, whether it is with love and kindness or anger and tension. The instinctive need for that feeling never leaves us—whether we are nine months or ninety. Our instinctive reaction is to massage our tummy when it is sore or to rub our forehead when we have a headache. Often a hug given with compassion and love is enough when words cannot be found to express how we are feeling.

You see, that deep need stays with us always, and we often want to revisit the childhood experience when we felt safe and secure in our mother's arms. It stays with us all, no matter how much we try to deny or ignore it, or how old we get. That lovely feeling of security as our mother picked us up after a fall or some such event. The injury usually wouldn't be too bad but our tears would last as long as possible, so we could make the hug and subsequent feeling of comfort go on and on indefinitely. Suddenly we'd feel safe and secure. We would sense that it was just the best place to be and yes—everything really was going to be okay as she gently and magically made our pain and tears go away. But time passes, we leave our childhood behind us and we become adults, so we don't like to "cry harder" or ask for a hug. But do you know what, nothing changes—the need is still there, that very same need as the crying distressed child who was able to express the feeling so easily with their tears. As an adult, however, it's often just not the right thing to do... simply because we are adults. I'm not saying that we should stay childlike forever and, of course, we do all have to grow up. I am saying that we should never ignore that deep feeling inside us that needs to be nurtured and loved—firstly by ourselves, and by doing so we are then able to allow others love and care for us too. I had a conversation with a friend who had just lost his Mum. His Dad was already dead so he was getting used to having no parents. He was a grown man but we both decided that no matter what age we are when our parents are gone, we somehow move up the ladder and lose that love that only they can give us. When they are alive we take that feeling of being loved and protected for granted—after all no one loves us so unconditionally as they do. Time, of course, is a great healer but it is so important to acknowledge these feelings so we can heal.

I feel, as I get older I walk my mother's walk. Everyday I feel moments where I am walking in her shoes and as the years go by I continue to get to know and understand my parents more and more. Sometimes people do a great job of hiding their vulnerable side. They give the impression of being totally in control, of being tough and decisive about everything—even considering it a sign of weakness to accept help or sympathy from anyone. What they are doing is building up a very tough "I'm okay" shell around themselves to hide their feelings. By continuing to do this they can become increasingly more and more defensive especially if they are shown the smallest bit of sympathy. To all intents and purposes they are what we often say about someone "their own worst enemy." Of course, that need to be nurtured is there, buried very deeply though. If then someone puts their arms around them with love it may not come as a surprise to see them cry like a baby.

Most of us go through life keeping a part of ourselves hidden. Not only from those around us but often from ourselves as well even though we have family and friends that we can share our feelings with. We deal with life's ups and downs on a daily basis so a lot of tensions build up .We think that the best way to cope is to keep going—by not letting our guard down, hence the fear of stopping for awhile and being alone. The fear being, that if we do this we won't be able to get up and go again. We subconsciously withdraw ever so slightly into our shell, while all the time there's a little part of us crying out for attention but it is so very deeply hidden. As soon as someone reaches out and places their hands on us to give comfort and love we instantly respond to that touch whether we want to or not. We are affected on many levels by their touch and embrace and so we find ourselves letting our guard down. By doing this we are able to let go of hidden emotions and tensions leaving us feeling lighter with the release, but also afraid, as we give in to how we are really feeling. Of course we feel scared, but by allowing ourselves become less fearful of our hidden depths they gradually lose their power over us and so we cope much better as we are more relaxed and peaceful. By doing this we are learning that it's okay to love and nurture ourselves once in a while by looking after our needs. When we allow some time and space for this, only then will we begin to feel some sense of being in harmony and at peace in the world we live in.

Gentle healing massage is a very powerful tool to enable us to do this, to help us like our own company—to take us out of our head and into our body, so making us more self-aware and at peace. As I said earlier, we allow tensions build up over time so we subconsciously hold ourselves taut and tense with the ever-increasing burden. This happens to us all as we live our normal lives. When the crisis then is a big one we hold ourselves even tighter as we try to deal with what is happening to us. A crisis such as cancer leaves us more vulnerable than ever as we struggle to keep it together. At a time such as this, never more is there a need to nurture, soothe and care for the little part of ourselves that we don't often show to everyone. The part of ourselves that our mother's love could so easily reach by her loving touch and embrace. So what better way to do this than through one of the simplest things, one of the oldest arts known to humanity—the healing power of touch. When I talk about massage at a time like this, I'm not talking about an experience where we are thumped and throttled on a massage table to a point where we discover muscles we never knew existed! I'm talking about finding a therapist who makes us feel totally at ease as she gently and tenderly massages our tense muscles. Allowing us to feel safe and free to be wherever we want to be inside our head so we can release whatever emotions come to the surface and not have to explain our sadness and tears. Instead allowing them to flow freely and by doing so helping us to get in touch with the little part of us that will blossom and grow from being lavished with so much attention. As it blossoms, we will feel more at one with ourselves and no longer feel the need to hide from who and what we really are.

This kind of massage, while it obviously works on a physical level with many advantages, is really working at a much deeper level as well. If the therapist and the environment are right the experience becomes one of healing that can facilitate the release of many blocked emotions and tensions. By this I mean an atmosphere that creates an environment of relaxation and security—that induces a feeling of calm as soon as we walk into the room. An atmosphere that subtly awakens all our senses, helping us to reach the state of well being that we all crave so much. We should immediately feel at ease with the décor and colours used, which if chosen wisely really should affect our mood in a positive way. Our sense of smell should be awakened as we inhale the wonderful soothing aromas of scented candles or oils burning. Combined with the sounds of healing relaxing music we should be well on our way to feeling calm as our senses do their work, sending the proper messages to our brain telling us to relax. As the therapist then massages our tense muscles we can be totally silent making the whole experience a spiritual one as we reconnect with our soul. In this stillness we find our very own sanctuary by just "being" and allowing our inner energies wake up and do their work. Being silent is such an important part of the whole experience as it allows us to be totally present with ourselves and by doing so we tap into those little voices that whisper between our thoughts.

The results are, of course, that we gradually over time learn to become more and more relaxed and in this relaxed state we cope much better with our daily lives. We become more accepting of what "is" and of what "will be." By acknowledging and listening to our own needs we become more self contained in the knowledge that we have all the resources inside us—once we nurture and care for ourselves with love. On the other hand, if we allow tensions to continue, we lose sight of that inner strength and of who we really are. We are constantly looking elsewhere for solutions to all our problems in life. Instead we should first and foremost look at ourselves...our strengths and weaknesses and so heal ourselves in the greatest way possible.

But life isn't always that simple or straightforward. In normal everyday living we are all plodding along as best we know how—hopefully getting it right some of the time at least. When we are then faced with a bigger crisis of any sort we are often totally thrown off balance. We are plodding along blindly having often lost the ability to know or sense what is right or wrong for us, even with the support of our family and friends. If we are lucky enough someone or something may come along to help us, to see what we may need. By their action or effect we are carried for a while until we are able to find our own way again. My family and I were completely thrown off balance following my diagnosis and even with their support I was still going along blindly a lot of the time, hoping and trusting that I was making some right decisions. My life was thrown into chaos so it was hard to be sure and decisive about anything. I was, however, lucky enough to have someone come along offering me her gift of regular massages for the duration of my chemotherapy. That person was Marian, and she certainly came along at the right time, introducing me to the amazing experience of massage. This was something I had never enjoyed before and would never have considered at that time, as I knew nothing about it's benefit's.

I have to be honest and tell you that I was more than a little nervous and self-conscious at the beginning. I had already lost a breast and having started my chemotherapy I was totally bald as well, so I was looking rather miserable to say the least. It was hard enough to look at myself in the mirror so the idea of someone else, that I didn't know very well, looking at my body was a bit daunting to say the least. I was beginning to wonder what advantages were to be gained, as I was feeling so self-conscious. I certainly didn't think I would be able to relax. The image that came to mind was of feeling exposed and laid bare, cringing as Marian worked over my poor battered body. I had no need to worry though as the reality was totally different. I was wrapped nicely in large towels that managed to cover my entire body, with only the part being worked on exposed at any one time. That in it'self allowed me to relax somewhat, but being "me" I felt uncomfortable with the long periods of silence and so I felt I had to keep a conversation going. Marian allowed me to chatter away to my heart's content but gradually over time I became more at ease with the silence and started to enjoy it as I forgot about my spare tyres, stretch marks... indeed everything and everyone. As I gave into this feeling more and more I felt my body relaxing and dissolving into the massage table thanks to Marian's gentle touch.

Learning to be quiet was a healing in it'self, not only for me but I'm sure for Marian as well as she didn't have to listen to my endless chatter about nothing in particular! Getting past those hang-ups about my body and allowing myself be alone with my thoughts was also very much part of the healing process. In this silence I found myself suppressing the urge to cry, suppressing it because I didn't want to appear foolish and because it frightened me with it's intensity. At the time I didn't understand what was happening, but of course I now know I was responding to being gently touched and to the compassion that went with the touch. A compassion that was giving me permission to just be myself and let go, knowing I didn't have to protect or fear upsetting anyone as I let my guard down for awhile. Being massaged was giving me the space to do this and gradually over time it enabled me to feel lighter and less burdened about the worry of my illness. With my doctor's consent I continued to have weekly massages for the duration of my treatment and I now like to include it as part of my lifestyle at least once a month or so. I look on it as my gift to myself, my nurturing time for me and I feel the benefit's enormously from being nice to myself now and again. My family feel the benefit's too, I might add, so they know what I like in my Christmas stocking. Of course, it's to their advantage as well as I don't rant and rave as much when I am nice and relaxed!

I am forever grateful to Marian for her thoughtfulness when I was ill. We all affect each other by our actions. Whether these actions are good or bad ones they have consequences for ourselves and those we come into contact with everyday. Consequences that vibrate on and on like a ripple in a pond. Thankfully the good usually overcome the bad and wins out in the end. Marian's good deed towards me had that effect. Because I enjoyed and gained so much from the experience I went on to train as a Massage Therapist myself. Nothing gives me greater pleasure than to pass on that experience to someone else. It is always a privilege to be allowed work with someone at such a personal level. I can honestly say that I nearly always gain as much from giving a massage as receiving one, especially when the person is comfortable enough to relax and be still. We all feel a need to fill silent spaces in conversation with useless chatter so I always like to give permission to whoever I am working with that it's okay to be quiet and I don't need to be entertained! Once they realise that the true healing begins. You see we all have our own ability to heal ourselves on many levels. Once we stop struggling and resisting, once we nurture and love the part of ourselves that cries for attention. When we listen and respond to that need our path to wellness has already begun.

Instead of seeing the rug being pulled from under us, we can learn to dance on the shifting carpet.

Thomas Crum

Music to Heal

CHEMOTHERAPY FOR ME brought good and bad days, on the bad days I had no choice but to rest. The overwhelming fatigue was such that my concentration became very poor. Watching television, reading or listening to the radio became activities that I could only tolerate for short periods. I was just too tired to do anything, and so lying in my bed my thoughts would run wild, filling my mind with all sorts of negative and dark self-pitying scenarios.

With no particular plan in mind, and also for the want of something better to do, I searched the house for some classical music I knew I had lying around somewhere. I started listening to them occasionally and found that instead of allowing my thoughts run in whatever direction they liked, the music seemed to help me detach myself from what was happening. Doing this made me more relaxed and at peace. I soon realised that if I listened to it more often it became much easier for me to switch off. Having no choice but to rest meant I had lots of time on my hands. So I was able to indulge myself, especially in the mornings, when the house was quiet. The music seemed to ease and soothe my mind and my love for it became fairly instant. Before long I was adding to my meagre collection of CD's and tapes, which I found quite easy to get everywhere. There is such a wide variety of this kind of music available in good music stores, chemists, health food shops, etc. It is so easily accessible to us all, and can be listened to anytime, anywhere or any place. Music combined with sounds of nature is particularly soothing and it really does have the ability to take you on a journey without ever leaving your house. By allowing ourselves time to listen to this kind of music on a regular basis, we give ourselves space to relax and our minds quickly learn to respond in a positive way. It's as though we are sending good signals to our thoughts to think "happy." I recently gave one of these CD's to a lady who was finding chemotherapy very difficult. It had a combination of music and sounds of the sea. I was delighted when she told me afterwards how much she enjoyed it. Her "bad" days became more tolerable because instead of lying in bed feeling miserable she found herself becoming totally absorbed in the music, and so things didn't seem as bad. She actually felt quite snug tucked up in a warm bed with all the various sounds taking her on a little journey inside her head. The sounds of waves and seagulls brought the sea to her, especially on the days when she couldn't get out for her much loved beach walks. It really is such a simple thing but so very powerful when used as part of one's healing journey.

It's all about making choices. If you have no choice but to slow down and rest due to circumstances such as illness, you do have a choice as to how to deal with that time. You can constantly moan and groan, wishing the time away, and so drive yourself and all those around you insane. Or you can choose to accept the time being given that you wouldn't normally have had, and use it in a positive way to catch up on favourite past-times, such as reading, etc. The outcome will stay the same, but by accepting what comes your way you will work towards that outcome in a much calmer state of mind. The same can be said about sitting in a traffic jam or doctor's surgery. Things won't move any faster if you rant and rave about the time wasted...

When you think about it, music affects us on many levels. It has the ability to make us laugh or cry. It can drive us insane. Indeed it has an energy all of it's own that can envelop us totally in it's beauty. Different parts of our body react to different sounds and rhythms so affecting us profoundly. Did you ever hear a song or piece of music being played that takes you right back to a distant memory in your past? The feelings, either sad or happy ones, can be so real as a result of the effect of the music. These awakened feelings can make you sad or happy all over again, about something, someone or some place in your past. A song associated with a long forgotten sun holiday can instantly conjure up images of sun, sea and sand. Of holiday romances, even smells of salty air and suntan lotions, making us relive the happy times in our life. On the other hand, a song from a sad time can make us revisit all that sadness once more. Doesn't this show us how powerful the energy of music really is? If our everyday thinking is influenced to such a degree by a particular piece of music, with no conscious effort on our part, imagine it's power then if it is used specifically to make us feel good and be more relaxed.

Some of the greatest songwriters and composers have created music that goes on and on. It is timeless and lives through generations of people young and old. This music has the ability to touch us deeply probably because it has come from a sad or happy place within that composer's own soul, and so communicates on a very deep level with ours. It may well have been his only means of self expression of what lies deep within his or her psyche so is it any wonder then that it affects us so much. Music is such a big part of spiritual life. Every day chants are sung by religious orders as a form of worship. This is by no means confined to the Christian tradition, but is a big part of every type of religion. In times gone by these chants were unaccompanied by music, but over the years a whole collection of written music has been composed. Along with the most meaningful and poetic words, it has the ability to reach a very deep part of us and so touch something deep inside our soul. Christmas carols being sung in Churches all over the world move many to tears that they cannot explain, tears that are allowed to flow freely and easily as the music and words embrace them in their beauty.

Nature too has it's own unique music that unfortunately for us we don't always hear. We only have to sit in a beautiful wood or stroll along a country lane to hear the most exquisite sounds of all. When we allow ourselves time and space to walk in a place of beauty we realise that nature sings a thousand songs and so we feel a deep connection to the universe all around us. All our senses come alive to the captive sounds of rustling leaves singing in the breeze, choirs of birds creating their own happy tunes. The lulling often-lonesome sounds of the sea as it ebbs and flows along the beach. Each season brings it's own music that is an irreplaceable work of art. The eerie silent sounds of winter making us feel quiet and reflective while the more uplifting sounds of spring and summer lifts our spirit's and has the ability to put a "pep" in our step.

So resolve to allow music, in whatever form you choose, become an instrument of healing in your life. Treat yourself to some of the many CD's available. Use it as a release of either great joy or deep sadness, as a means of self-expression of what lies deep inside your soul. Allow it to reach down inside you, easing and soothing your thoughts. Allow it give you permission to just "be" and so really experience what you are feeling. Tears will flow naturally and easier and so will be cathartic and healing. Listen to it anytime, any place, anywhere. There are no rules, it's your choice, wherever you like and whatever type of music you like. Just trust your own instinct and so feel the freedom in creating beauty and peace, where sometimes everything feels dark and full of despair. Allow the music of your own choice go on to work it's magic on your soul again and again.

We have a pharmacy inside us that is absolutely exquisite. It makes the right medicine, for the precise time, for the right target organ...with no side effects.

Deepak Chopra.

Yoga, Candle Gazing, Bubble Baths...Bliss!

I LEARNED the most unexpected things at my yoga class. I joined it when I was coming to the end of my chemo, not really knowing too much about it. What I had in mind were lots of nice gentle stretches and exercises to help ease my tired and stressed body, which I was badly in need of I might add. There were plenty of exercises and stretching which were really very nice. But there was so much more to the class that I certainly wasn't expecting. Things like learning to breathe properly, which I thought I was already doing automatically since birth but obviously not, according to Sadie our yoga teacher. Things like gazing at a candle flame until my eyes watered so much that I just wanted to go to sleep. Things like directing my thoughts to different parts of my body sending it lots of healing energy. This energy then bringing my awareness to those areas that needed healing as I slowly and gently stretched and eased my sore muscles telling them to relax and be well. Just in case we forgot how to create that feeling between classes we were told things like how to turn our bathing experience into one of complete relaxation and peace...just by adding lots of scented oils-loads of time and a few candles. Absolute heaven, I might add, and you don't even have to leave your own home to do it. Mind you the first time I did this my family became concerned when I seemed to be missing for ages especially when they realized the light was off as well. I was brought back to reality pretty quickly with shouts of "what on earth are you doing in there in the dark!" They do give me funny looks sometimes but I think they are used to me by now and if it stops me from nagging them too much they are even happy to buy the candles and oils for me! Anything for a quiet life I suppose.

There are numerous different types of yoga classes available but as I'm not an expert I can't really discuss them. All I do know is that when I was recovering from cancer I didn't need anything too strenuous or energetic, instead I needed a class where the emphasis was more on relaxation and thankfully that's exactly what I joined. As there are so many types of yoga classes, I suppose the thing to do is decide what it is you want and then get advice about what suit's you. Marian, who had been keeping me sane with her wonderful massages recommended this particular class to me. I was an emotional and physical wreck as I came to the end of my chemotherapy so it was exactly what I needed. The whole emphasis of our class was one of relaxation and healing. Sadie, our teacher, acted as our guide allowing us to do as little or as much as we wanted. The room was usually full of people and yet it was so easy to be in our own space as we were gently led through a series of stretches, breathing exercises, candle gazing, and then relaxation/visualisation. Usually by that stage there were lots of snores coming from different corners of the room and it was often difficult to physically get up and go home. Over time the benefit's of this weekly discipline begin to become apparent as we are training ourselves to relax. We are learning many techniques to help us deal with stressful situations and as with any discipline it does gradually get easier to do so. Once you start a yoga class you realise that there is so much more to it than mere exercise. As I said earlier I learned so many things that I wasn't expecting to. Our body has a natural energy flow that keeps us healthy and well. This energy flow does get blocked for any number of reasons such as tension and stress. Yoga stretches that are long and slow help to get rid of a lot of this tension. As we stretch our bodies from top to bottom we learn to concentrate on our inner organs at the same time and so we release many blockages allowing our body's natural energy flow to continue.

A lot of the movements were devised from observation of animals since they appeared to be expert at relaxation and their movements involve minimum effort. Lovely poses such as 'the cat' and 'the cobra' have such wonderful healing benefit's for our body and the movements are done exactly as these animals would do. Poses such as 'salute to the sun' were meant to be just that…saluting the sun at sunrise and sunset…Again as I have said over and over again, nature and animals have so much to teach us if we only stop for a while and observe. The deep breathing that is part of this process helps us to increase our oxygen levels. As we develop this technique all negative thoughts flow out with the breath and as we concentrate on our rhythm and movements we slip into a meditative state and so our minds are at rest

As I said earlier, I thought I knew how to breathe properly, after all we do it automatically from birth until death. Human life actively begins with the first breath and ends with the final sigh. We depend on the quantity and the quality of the oxygen inhaled and on the way it is inhaled.

Unfortunately, we don't always get it right and as a result our physical and emotional systems suffer. Our breathing is unique in that it works automatically but we can consciously control it, unlike the functions of our internal organs that work without us even being aware of them. Something wonderful happens when we bring our attention to our breath. Our self-awareness increases and so tension that is lurking in the most unlikely places is released. I often went along to my yoga class thinking that I was fairly relaxed and calm but as soon as my body started to react to the breathing exercises I'd discover areas of tension that I hadn't noticed before. One of nature's best regulating forces for relaxation is breathing so isn't it a pity that we don't make more of an effort to do it properly. Imagine the feeling we get when faced with a sudden shock—our breathing is totally disrupted, becoming shallow and irregular. Nature however, being the wonderful teacher it is, means that we usually give a huge big sigh, which results in regulating our breath as the muscles are forced to relax with the sigh. You see then how it is linked to our emotional system...when we are excited or afraid we breathe more rapidly, when we are calm, so too is our breath.

Yoga shows us that vital link between mind body and spirit, which we can all control to our own advantage by increasing our awareness of our breath. It teaches us, that instead of taking little shallow breaths we should breathe deeply enough to feel our abdominal wall rising. As we continue to put this into practice it becomes the most natural thing in the world and gets easier and easier. Each week we learned then to combine this natural breathing process with our gentle stretches, which managed to make us feel totally relaxed. The remaining part of the class involved candle gazing. This means literally what it says...each of us lying or sitting comfortably in a semi dark room while gazing at a candle flame. This really had the effect of allowing us to be totally in our own space even though the room was full of people. We were then gently led into a guided meditation that managed to send most of us to sleep as we directed only good and positive thoughts all around our body.

As I came to the end of my chemotherapy I really was an emotional and physical wreck. I had worked really hard to keep it together but as I was physically exhausted it was hard to keep being constantly positive. The reality was, of course, that I was very depressed and thankfully I heeded my doctor's advice [with difficulty I might add] so I commenced a course of anti-depressants. It was without doubt the best thing I could have done as it gave me back my much-needed clarity and focus that I had lost. I was then able to look at ways to help me get my life back on track and joining my yoga class was one of the things I did.

If I had continued in my depressive state I would never have had the energy or focus to even begin thinking about joining anything new. You see I had a fair idea of the benefit's of caring for myself and of being relaxed but when you are depressed you lose sight of all that knowledge. Unfortunately, as nurses or anyone in the caring profession, we sometimes find it hard to look for help. We are used to being the carer and so it can be hard to have the roles reversed. Not only that, we can see it as a sign of weakness on our part. We have been giving advice and caring for so long it's as though we should have all the answers and coping skills. But we are human beings first and foremost, just the same as anyone else. Thankfully the antidepressants gave me the chance to explore and learn my own set of coping skills so after a few months I was able to come off them without too much effort. Joining the yoga class made me feel I was doing something for myself and so I was regaining some sense of control at a time when my world was crazy.

We all want peace in our lives and we often have all the knowledge to attain that peace. As this can involve changing lifelong habit's and indeed a whole way of living we don't always have the courage or will to make up our minds to do so. If we do decide to take some control it does take effort and discipline. Joining things like a yoga or meditation class, or going for a massage or any type of healing session isn't going to change things instantly as much as we might like it to. Also the instructor/therapist isn't going to solve all our problems. Instead he or she will act as the facilitator allowing us to tap into our own healing and by doing so we are then learning our own set of coping skills. It's by no means a quick fix solution like swallowing a pill; it does involve a lot of effort, discipline and constant awareness. The thing is though, that once we start to change and begin to take a few small steps however small they seem, we will then get the courage to take a few more. And so our journey on this rocky road will get easier and less burdened.

When we experience pure silence in the mind, the body becomes silent also. And in that field of silence, healing is much more efficient.

Deepak Chopra

Meditation...The Silent Teacher

EVERY TIME I STARTED TO WRITE this chapter I seemed to hit a brick wall. I made numerous attempts but I never seemed to get it right. I couldn't figure out what was wrong...after all I had learned how to do it and I had all the knowledge, so why on earth wasn't I able to get the message down on paper. I was beginning to get a bit sick of the whole thing and then out of the blue somehow it dawned on me. Okay, so I knew all the techniques but in reality I wasn't doing it myself, I was telling everyone else how wonderful it was but I wasn't practicing what I preached! I had been so very disciplined meditating every day but somehow I'd let it slip and had allowed myself just fall out of the habit. Isn't that so typical of all our lives. We know all the answers, we have read all the books but if we don't apply it to ourselves we are just wasting our time. There really is no such thing as not having time. We all use that as our excuse but if we really want to we can make a space for ourselves in our day with just the slightest bit of effort and discipline. But I can't emphasise it enough, we do have to consciously make that effort every day over and over again.

Have you ever found yourself in the middle of a seemingly endless workload and thought to yourself there has to be more to life than this? Have you ever felt totally overwhelmed with the whole range of responsibilities that have taken over your life? Responsibilities that seem to leave so little time for anything else while all the time at the back of your mind you just know there has to be a deeper meaning to it all. If we are all honest we will admit to having some or all of these feelings from time to time. It certainly doesn't mean we are depressed or selfish even though it may appear that way, especially when we seemingly have it all in the material sense at least. That yearning can't be filled by any amount of material wealth, it's a longing for something unexplainable within ourselves. It's that feeling we experience when we are in a place of natural beauty, maybe a beautiful forest or overlooking a vast ocean. The sheer beauty is so immense and powerful we feel a sense of something deeply affecting us that cannot be explained. We feel a connection with the universe. The beauty all around makes us instinctively know there really is something more after all, that we are such a small part of something so much bigger than who we are.

The beauty of nature touches our very soul in a way that nothing else can. It's a feeling we want to hold on to but it seems to slip from our grasp as much as we try to keep it alive. That feeling has touched and awakened our soul, our very essence, the center of our being. The yearning to hold onto that feeling is our soul crying out to be nurtured and fulfilled. It's letting us know that it has always been there, reminding us of our true identity. Unfortunately, who we really are has a tendency to get lost in our mad crazy world of endless work and deadlines.

We are all inclined to lose sight of that identity, our soul and so we run the risk of thinking that the image we portray to the world is who we really are. We build our lives on our outside identity whether it's our career or role as mother father sister or brother. We identify ourselves by these titles, which can cause us endless inner conflict. As we lose sight of our essential nature we really do become lost and confused souls, so that feeling continues to invade our psyche. Who we really are is deep within us all. It has always been there but we do need to find our own way to rediscover that sense of self. Once we do this we must keep that feeling alive and nurtured. A lot of the pain and sadness we experience is a loss of our identity and unfortunately the concept of spiritual awareness is getting more and more lost in our advanced technological world. Silence is the means of holding onto that sense of spirituality, of nurturing and recognising our soul.

Learning to meditate gives us the time we need to create our own quiet space. However, we are often inclined to feel uncomfortable, or even afraid of silence, and we will do anything to avoid being alone with ourselves. In a world that appears to have gone mad, finding our core of silence is like recapturing our inner serenity and peace all over again. This silence allows our soul to rise to the surface and so makes everything clear and simple for us. Meditation can instantly conjure up all sorts of complicated images of monks in various stages of trance like states. It is an ancient art after all and has been part of the East Indian tradition for thousands of years. The thing is though it doesn't have to be at all complicated. With a little effort we can include it in our day-to-day lives with huge advantages to our well-being and ourselves.

You maybe surprised to know that we are already doing it time and time again with no conscious effort on our part.

You know you are doing it when you lose track of time, you're not asleep and are aware of where you are but you seem to have fallen into a vacant space inside your head. It can happen anywhere or anytime. Maybe at a meeting or ceremony of any sort, or sitting gazing at a fire burning where you just become absorbed in the dancing flames. I remember, as a child, often lying on our lawn on a summer's day drifting off somewhere inside my head and having to consciously shake myself back to reality, I wouldn't have been asleep but would feel rested and relaxed afterwards. I suppose the term daydreaming is fairly apt to describe what I was doing! Moments like this happen to us all and even if they are accidental they are still good for us. Of course it would be even better if we consciously decide to learn how to do it properly and include it as a regular part of our day. By doing this we then gain the benefit's in lots of ways in our lives. Silence really is a great teacher and by resting our minds we are able to think more clearly, helping us to get in touch with our inner calmness that unites our body mind and spirit. Our physical body sustains us continuously and we should learn to sit and listen to it's needs and inner intelligence. To maintain our health we must try to be in harmony with ourselves and by doing so we are then in harmony with others and the universe. When we are out of harmony we lose direction and so leave ourselves open to any number of ailments.

Disease isn't called 'dis...ease' for nothing, it's exactly as it says...'disturbed ease,' which of course means that we are sick in some way. I was certainly out of harmony with myself when I was faced with a cancer diagnosis. I was totally thrown off balance and I very quickly learned there was no running away from the reality of it all. My thoughts were running wild inside my head and I was desperately in need of some peace and calm in my life. Learning to meditate was one of the most empowering things I did at that time. As I said before, throughout my chemotherapy, I had already started to tap into my own inner potential and strength through massage and yoga etc. I was anxious to learn more so when my chemotherapy was finished I joined a meditation class. I was fast becoming the ultimate 'therapy junkie' after all! Doing these things was helping me to learn and realise the benefit's of silence. And, of course I was also learning to be comfortable with it as well, which was amazing as I am inclined to talk a lot .As I peeled back more and more layers I was rediscovering my true potential and hidden strength. I believe that we never lose that part of us but we do have to relearn and rediscover it again and again.

So how do we do it? What does it involve and what does it feel like? Well, for starters as there are so many forms of meditation, it's about finding a way that suit's you and as we are all individuals everyone's experience will be unique and personal for them. My experience involved joining a class at our local holistic centre where we learned to meditate with our class leader Rex Dunlop. It usually began by learning to sit comfortably with our spine straight and feet firmly on the ground. The importance of this posture being that we were relaxed and comfortable but yet alert and aware. If we were lying down or slouched in our chairs we would prob- ably fall asleep and that's not what meditation is all about. A guided relaxation followed with our awareness focused on our breathing allowing our body to release all of it's ten- sions and stress. In this relaxed state we would then just sit in silence, doing nothing, just being, not thinking or forcing it, but letting any thoughts that came to mind float right out again. The aim of the exercise would be that as our physi- cal body relaxed our mind would gradually become clear, blank, and free from thoughts. It really is surprising how very busy our minds are and it's not until we stop and become aware of this that we realise how hard it can be to sit for even a few minutes in silence and stillness. The first few times we do it maybe quite difficult, as our heads are full of all sorts of useless thoughts, which clutter up our thinking. Thoughts as mundane as "what's for dinner today" or "did I remember to lock the door!" This can be frustrating as we can feel that not a lot is being achieved but with practice it does get easier if, instead of forcing it we just acknowledge these thoughts and then let them float out again. We may only manage a few minutes at the beginning but over time we will automatically sit for longer. While initially we maybe restless eventually we do slip into that blank space where time doesn't exist. We are awake but are totally relaxed and at peace in the stillness.

If we are doing it correctly our body should feel so comfortable without us even being aware of it and so our emotions will be at peace. Meditation is not thinking, but instead it's about giving our mind a break, creating our own sacred space and listening to the silence between our thoughts. Usually our minds are so full that there is no room for thinking clearly. This rest is as beneficial to it as sleep is to the body. Everyone finds his or her own way to achieve this stillness, there is no right or wrong. Some use things like music, nature or meditation tapes to create that sacred space within themselves. Once you find that space it gets easier to tap into it no matter where you are or what situation you are in. You know it's always there if you need it. The benefit's are endless and it can be what keeps you centred in the middle of all the chaos.

Meditation gets us in touch with our own inner essence and provides a constant communication with our soul, so satisfying that longing need that we all experience from time to time. It allows us to tap into our creative side which we all have in various ways but may not even know or realise it. Ways such as music, writing, painting, gardening etc. The list is endless. That creativity then helps to keep our soul nurtured and fulfilled, as it's our means of true self-expression of who we really are. This is often not the image we portray to the world, I might add, so of course it may frighten us a little. You only have to look at the work of some great artists to see how they use their talent and creativity as a means of expression. Their aim is not so much about how rich and famous they become. It has more to do with achieving a sense of fulfilment and inner joy from their art through whatever medium they use.

Creativity is as natural as breathing. When we do it, we explore who we really are. That power enters us and we spontaneously create. In this state what we create is beautiful. Like the uncomplicated child who freely and without fear or hang-ups expresses their thoughts in the most simple and basic artwork. That form of expression comes directly from their soul and so it speaks to ours, touching us in a very deep way. The answers are within us all, if we only stop and listen we will be guided in a way that is right for us.

As we continue to make it a part of our everyday routine we keep that feeling alive and we feel truly at peace within ourselves. It shouldn't be a separate part of our lives but over time it should become our whole life. The aim of learning to meditate and putting it into practice is that we should have a heightened awareness so that every thought we have is in harmony with the universe around us. I am still learning and I have to constantly discipline myself to make it a regular part of my day-to-day life, which of course I don't always do. For me learning to meditate means that no matter how mad my world appears to be I know I always have my very own sacred space to fall back on. When I go into that space it's like coming home again and again and it always feels so very safe and right. That inner peace manifests it'self in many physical ways as I feel more relaxed and in tune with my own body and it's needs. I feel blessed for having found and tapped into these inner strengths and also that I now recognise what that yearning and longing is all about. That I am a small part of something so much bigger than me, and yes there is more to "me" than just flesh and bones. As I accept this I no longer feel the need to constantly control and plan my life. I don't allow myself get bogged down in endless worry about all the "what if's." By worrying I am once again trying to control my future instead of just living in the present. There really is a freedom in this letting go as I accept more what comes, knowing I will be gently and lovingly led along in a way that is right for me. Whether we worry or not things usually do work out anyway because we are constantly led by our intuition and conscience. The thing is to give ourselves the space of stillness to listen and so follow our own unique path.

Champions aren't made in gyms. Champions are made from something they have deep inside them, a desire, a dream, and a vision. They have to have the skill and the will. But the will must be stronger than the skill.

Muhammad Ali, Boxing Champion

Visualisation/Mental Imagery...All in the Mind?

OUR IMAGINATION CAN TAKE US ANYWHERE we want to go. It is a language and gift that we all possess and using it can be like an adventure, an inner journey with absolutely no restrictions or limitations but ourselves. We only have to watch a child at play to see how real it's power is. They can create all sorts of wonderful scenarios and games using little else but their imagination, so making their fun and enjoyment a magical and mysterious experience. As adults we don't always allow ourselves that freedom but we still use it everyday without realizing it. Our natural imagination helps us to create images of things we would like or wish for...maybe a new home, holiday, car, even a perfect body image. The list is endless and of course if we want and wish for something bad enough it does often happen. It's amazing where we can go inside our heads and even more amazing the images we can create. Our thoughts and imagination are a language after all and are so very powerful, so powerful in fact that if we realized it we would never think a negative thought again.

We unconsciously create negative and positive thoughts all the time. These thoughts affect us on many levels, they have the ability to make us at peace with our day-to-day lives and they have the ability to make us sick. If we are sick they really can influence our road to wellness or at least how we choose to endure our illness. We don't set out to make ourselves ill, but our psychological state really does affect our well-being. There is more to 'us' than just what we see. The concept of unity of mind body and spirit cannot be ignored, especially when faced with a serious illness. If we continue to put ourselves under pressure we do leave ourselves wide open to any number of ailments, which can effect us in any number of ways. If then we are faced with a serious illness and we acknowledge that our emotions and thoughts have played their part in this illness we can then realize the huge power they have. Instead of getting into a blind panic we should see that if they have the ability to make us ill, well then surely they can be directed in such a way as to make us healthy and well. At the very least they can influence how we deal with that illness.

Visualisation/mental imagery is a technique where we can train our imagination in a positive way to help with our healing process. By doing this we create an image of what we want or would like in our life. The only thing necessary is our desire for that wish and the only restriction is ourselves. Now before you begin to think that it's complicated and difficult, remember, you are already doing it everyday with daily wishes, prayers and hopes for the future. It just needs a little fine-tuning and direction. When we are ill, visualisation/mental imagery involves training our thought process in a way to create images of healing for our body. This healing can take on many forms and can happen on many levels. It can create hope where there has been hopelessness; it can create a positive and peaceful environment where there has been fear and negativity. This environment can then allow all sorts of physical healing to happen.

In the early stages of my illness my thoughts were totally negative...as far as I was concerned I had cancer so that was that. I certainly didn't think I had any choice but to leave myself in the hands of the medical profession's prescribed course of treatment and hope for the best. Now I didn't give that impression to everyone but that was the way my deep thought process was working. Someone had given me a book called *Getting Well Again* (available on amazon.co.uk website) by Carol and Stephanie Simonton and with nothing better to do lying in bed one miserable day I decided to see what it had to say. We should never underestimate the power of the written word as reading that book had a huge impact on my way of thinking. It made me feel there was something I could do for myself after all, making me realize that I wasn't quite as powerless as I thought.

It discussed the psychological aspects of our illness and how our thoughts really do influence our ability to heal and to make ourselves ill in the first place. They back up their claims with numerous case studies that are hard to ignore... like the man with inoperable throat cancer who changed the whole course of his illness through being thought how to use mental images of his white cells attacking his cancer. He went on to live for many years after that. This was one of many such stories that made me give myself a good shake. They also talk about personality types that get certain illnesses and I have to say that I very quickly recognized myself and all my fussy organized ways. Lots of guidelines were given showing you how to visualise and use mental imagery as part of this process. As I had lots of time lying in bed feeling sorry for myself I felt I had nothing to lose by trying to put some of what they said into practice. It was certainly a better option than lying there wallowing in self-pity and getting more and more miserable by the day. The personal stories in the book had such an effect that I had an overwhelming urge to start taking back some control of my life...if these people could do it well then why couldn't I?

So in the privacy of my own home I began my very own journey. Without leaving my bedroom I let my imagination flow as freely and uninhibited as child I once was. I created all sorts of images in my head of lovely healing energy coming my way. I created images of my chemotherapy, not as a toxic drug but a healing liquid flowing around my body killing anything that shouldn't be there. Instead of saying 'this is going to make me sick' I would focus on the fact that it was going to make me well again. Once I got started there was no stopping me. I had an imaginary army at work with me at all times, they were with me always and gave me a strong sense of being looked after and in control. I used the wonderful energy of music to help me on this journey. Listening to the wonderful sounds of nature helped me wander in places of beauty in my mind when I hadn't the physical energy to even leave my bed. Every chance I had, I told myself I was getting well and created an affirmation that I constantly used every day. This affirmation was my own personal one..."my body is totally healed, I have the power to keep myself well" Of course, we can all make one that suit's our own individual needs because after all our own needs are uniquely personal to us.

Doing these simple things gave me back some sense of control, which was so very empowering and uplifting. I felt stronger and more in control as I trained my mind to think in a good way. It was as though I was detoxing and cleansing my mind of all the negative and toxic thoughts.

We often cleanse our physical selves but don't do the same with our emotions. Of course I didn't know if it was having any impact on my cancer but I did know one thing it was better than lying there feeling sorry for myself. Instead of constantly worrying I was becoming more relaxed and was able to switch off much easier than ever before. We do have some choices to make when we are faced with a crisis and we can choose whether we want to be miserable or happy. It can be easy to give in to the misery but it is so much better to make the effort to be happy. By harbouring bitterness and unhappiness we are only hurting ourselves again and again. It's not enough to do right and say we are positive, we must think right and think positive and every positive thought we have has a good effect not only on ourselves but those around us as well.

I continued along in my own way all through my chemo and when I joined meditation and yoga, guided imagery was a very big part of the class. Gradually, over time, it became a way of life to me as I became more and more aware of my thought process. Learning to meditate showed me how much more powerful thought process is if we learn to relax first. As our body relaxes our minds become more receptive and so we continue to work daily miracles in our lives. It really is hard to ignore the connection between our thoughts and feelings on one hand and our immune system on the other. Guided imagery helps us to gain access to our inner imagination creating an environment of healing and positive energy. Every positive thought has a good effect and when we are faced with a serious illness we need these positive thoughts more than ever. I can't emphasize enough that it's not enough to say we are positive we must learn to really really think positively. Of course the idea of this may seem difficult but it's about making a choice, wallowing in self-pity or learning to be happy. Now it's easy enough to see which is the best option but it does take a little work and every day we have to reaffirm those positive thoughts all over again. They don't just happen as those negative thoughts are never too far away. If this is proving to be very difficult it is important to acknowledge that we can't always do it alone and so we may need help to find and tease out the underlying cause of our problem. Maybe talking to a counsellor we are able to get right under the fear that holds us back from being at peace with ourselves and by doing so we clear the way for creating all those positive mental images. You see no matter what is going on in our lives we do have complete control over our attitude and how we choose to deal with it. In every situation we face there is a lesson to be learned. It's a blessing if we learn that lesson and it is good to be tested because it's from these tests that we grow and develop. When we come through these difficult times we are able to look back and see how much stronger we have become from the experience. Once we see this it is also important to leave it in the past, acknowledge the wisdom we have attained and most importantly move on bringing that knowledge with us on our journey through life.

If you are reading this and are faced with a serious illness remember there is no such thing as false hope. It's important to be realistic but it's also important not to be totally pessimistic. Hope is essential, whatever stage you are at, even if there is no hope of recovery there is still always something to realistically aim for. Without hope we would all become totally depressed and lifeless. I have seen people who were terminally ill hoping to last long enough to see a loved one maybe get married, give birth or graduate from college. Such was their determination that they often lasted way past the time predicted by their doctors. We all have the wonderful gift of our imagination. It's an essential and important part of us and is usually not being used to it's full potential. Remind yourself of your childhood and all those amazing games you played...of all that you wished for and all that came true. Don't be afraid to let that imagination flow again and make your wishes and hopes for the future real and powerful. If you have cancer create an image of your own choice. Maybe an image of those cancer cells being attacked and overpowered by your immune system. You can be as creative as you want; I liked to imagine a little army of soldiers marching along zapping anything that shouldn't be there. It's totally up to you what image you want to create and remember there are no limitations but yourself. If you are finding it difficult and feel that you can't do it on your own why not join a meditation class or one that teaches you how to visualise. There are many books available on the subject and many tapes to help you train those thoughts. Most importantly be gentle with yourself and always be aware that healing can and does happen day after day and never ever give up hope.

So if you have become a statistic and joined thousands of others who have cancer remember no two people are the same and no two people are ill in the same way. You are unique; you are alive and in control of how you choose to live your life no matter what the doctors say. Even if your illness is terminal you are here today. You are alive and we are all in charge of our lives until the very end. We think that healing is something prescribed for us and of course this is partly right. I, for one, will never underestimate the power of modern medicine. But by taking an active part in our own healing as well as all the prescribed care we really do become a force to be reckoned with.

When the first baby laughed for the first time, the laugh broke into a thousand pieces and they all went skipping about, and that was the beginning of fairies.

James M. Barrie

It's Okay to Laugh

I READ SOMEWHERE that laughter and fun are holidays for our soul as it's only through sadness and suffering that we learn our greatest lessons. Emotional pain after all does have a way of screaming at us whether we like it or not. Now I do agree that it's through our difficulties in life that we learn. They really are opportunities in disguise for spiritual growth. Once we acknowledge that we will be encouraged by our success and strengthened by our failures. I'm all for learning and exploring—but do you know what, I love a break from it as well and I don't like being forever serious. So on one hand I can be very philosophical and questioning about life [perhaps too much so at times!] but also I can get such enjoyment and satisfaction from light hearted humour and fun by finding ways to smile and be happy. Then again isn't that what life is all about—finding happiness in the midst of all the ups and downs of our hectic lives. Sadly though I'm beginning to think that we are losing our sense of humour and our ability to smile has diminished somewhat. Lost in our endless busy routines and deadlines...now

I've just had a thought about that—maybe that's why they are called "dead" lines!

I was in a Dublin shopping centre with my daughter at Christmas and the crowds were driving me absolutely insane. I decided to abandon any hope of shopping, which didn't bother me too much, I might add, as I hate it anyway! My daughter went her way buying her presents while I found myself a seat to just sit and relax watching the world go by. Now remember it was "the season of good will" and all that…but looking around me there were very few smiling faces. In fact I could even go so far as to say that most people looked fairly stressed and miserable caught up in their own world and shopping lists. The whole place was full of families out for their Christmas shopping which of course is meant to be a "happy" day. As with a lot of things in life it doesn't always go to plan and can often end up going pear shaped with the stress of it all. I do know what I'm talking about now because I've been there! Wives looked as if they could kill their husbands—as the husbands looked positively bored with expressions that said it was the last place they wanted to be. Mothers were trying to smile and be nice to their children while really they looked ready to abandon them in the nearest children's home. All in all very few made eye contact with anyone in case they'd have to say hello or maybe even smile. If I did happen to say "hello" or "excuse me," I was usually met with some strange questioning looks as if I was a bit odd to say the least.

Isn't it such a strange scenario? Everyday in crowded places such as that shopping centre all these people are in such close proximity to each other, but it's as though they are all miles apart. One of my good friends is a naturally friendly person, if she is in a queue or near anyone in a restaurant or public transport, etc., she always says hello to whoever is near her. I can assure you she's perfectly normal with no hidden agenda's, but people just can't accept her openness. Someone once turned to her and very suspiciously said "do I know you?" as if she had an ulterior motive for saying hello to them. Isn't it sad that we have to be so careful and wary of everybody but I suppose it is understandable in today's world. I'm not saying we should go around smiling and talking constantly to everyone we meet. We would surely get ourselves into some sticky situations. Not only that we may find ourselves being committed to the nearest institution... for our own safety, I might add, which may not be part of our overall plan for our lives. I do think the occasional smile is worth that risk though, don't you?

So let's be honest here, when was the last time you had a really good laugh? Now I mean a laugh that goes right through your whole body making you shake as your belly aches and tears come to your eyes. It's such a good feeling isn't it, and leaves such a lovely afterglow as if you are plugged into a good and positive energy...but the trouble is we don't do it often enough. We would certainly make more of an effort if we were told that laughter and happy thoughts create positive changes in our body. Changes that result in making us feel better, by stimulating our feel good hormones and so enhancing our immune system. On the other hand negative emotions and stress have the very opposite effect— lowering our natural fight back mechanism exactly at the time when we need all the help we can get. Unfortunately, at a time like that when we are facing sickness or stress of any sort the last thing we may feel like doing is laughing, and if we do we are left with a vague feeling of guilt about doing so. A friend of mine lost her son tragically some years ago. She told me that for a long time afterwards, whenever she found herself laughing or being somewhat happy in any way, she felt overwhelmed with guilt. It was as though she wasn't being true to his memory as in that few minutes of laughter she forgot her sadness, and so forgot him as well. That guilt stayed with her for a long time but gradually she came to realise that it was okay to have moments of happiness and he certainly wouldn't want her constantly weighed down with grief. She continued to grieve in her own way accepting the happy and sad moments as part of the process to heal.

The thing is you see, we need to consciously give ourselves permission to laugh no matter how bad things seem. I'm not saying that we should deny the emotions that come with any stressful event in our lives. I do think that in the midst of all the pain and tears there is nothing wrong with allowing ourselves moments of laughter. It is by no means taking from the seriousness of our situation but it really does act as a release of built up tensions and stress. The very fact that we allow ourselves to, is in it'self a gift, and haven't we often heard people saying, "if I didn't laugh I'd cry," because really they both have much the same effect on our body—acting as a release mechanism. You see, laughing and crying are very similar. They both release tears and sometimes they even get mixed up. We can start crying and end up laughing, or start laughing and end up crying. We can find ourselves laughing when we should be crying...and find ourselves crying when we should be laughing. We have cried tears of joy and then again we have cried tears of sadness so it's sometimes hard to know what the tears are for. I talk in the chapter "The Circle Of Life" about when we were student nurses faced with death for the first time; we were in a whole new situation beyond our understanding. In trying to deal with it, our emotions got all mixed so we would react by saying something funny to lighten the mood and inevitably we would all end up laughing. Slightly hysterically I might add just because we didn't know what else to do.

You see laughter acted as our defence mechanism by delaying facing something so great as death. That need gradually diminished as we came to terms with dealing with death and dying as part of our role as nurses—thankfully I might add as we wouldn't have been able to do our jobs properly if we continued that way. Soon after my diagnosis, when I was really struggling to deal with what had happened to me I called into my place of work for coffee one morning. I know I hadn't even begun to come to terms with my diagnosis. So what did I do? I made light of the whole thing just in case anyone would get too serious and ask me something that I hadn't even asked myself yet. I set the tone of the conversation by directing it my way, making jokes about my hair loss, wig, etc., etc. and as a result we all ended up laughing for most of the time. When I left, the girls probably thought I was so very positive but the reality was that I cried all the way home. Crying from the strain I had put on myself to hide from what I was really feeling. It was the very same as being the student nurse all over again when faced with death for the first time and not knowing how to deal with it. You see laughter is all very well as long as it is genuine and from the heart—not hiding the real feelings underneath. But we are all only human—we don't always get it right and a lot of the time we are trying to survive as best we can.

So let's imagine we have been told that laughter is better than any of the prescribed drugs on the market, that it has the ability to enhance our wellbeing and can even contribute to our getting well when we are sick. The only snag being that we can't get it on prescription so we have to find our own way to create and then channel it's wonderful energy. Well then, how do we go about doing that properly? The first thing is we should do it because we mean it—not because we want to hide our real feelings. We should actively seek out positive and happy people and on the other hand avoid those who are constantly focussing on the negative aspects of life. Let them do their moaning somewhere else, we don't need them in our lives. They will only drag us down and so stop the natural flow of happiness that we are so busy trying to create. We should create plenty of light comic relief by watching funny films, reading funny books...sharing jokes and funny stories with friends and family. We certainly shouldn't be afraid to laugh no matter how bad things seem as our sense of humour really will help us through those difficult times. Being able to laugh at ourselves is important as we stop taking life too seriously, for a while at least. I believe my sense of humour has helped me so much throughout my life and never more so than when I got sick. It did get lost and confused for a while but thankfully it came back. Our sense of humour is something we should hold on to at all costs. If we don't have one we should make an effort to develop one, as it is good to lighten up and laugh at ourselves every now and then.

It really is the best "chill pill" available to us. As this sense of humour becomes more and more apparent, it becomes an unending two-way source of energy for ourselves and those we meet. True happiness inspires others to laugh too and so we attract and give out positive vibes. After all, we cannot give without receiving and we cannot receive without giving. Life really is like a mirror, smile and it smiles back but moan and it will moan right back!! Now if we are being really good and doing all this properly we should at this stage have our own constant source of laughter medicine that doesn't even cost us a penny. We don't even have to bottle it for others as they will naturally absorb it from us and then continue to pass it on and on; isn't it just great and it's free! Now I wonder why the drug companies haven't copped on and tried to market this product somehow. But sure why would they bother, after all they want to make loads of money and I'm sure they have realised by now that we can all create our own at no cost at all.

By obsessing over perfection we miss the uniqueness of the moment. The world was created imperfectly so that we could love it for what it is and love ourselves for what we are.

Nature's Blessings and Seasonal Lessons

WE ALL HAVE OUR OWN PERSONALITY. No matter how much we may try to change ourselves we are born with a personality that is unique and individual to us. It is after all who we are and it influences our physical mental and emotional being. As human beings we do have lots of similar trait's but wouldn't the world be so very boring if we were all totally the same. Our personality and rhythm influence every aspect of our lives and so the important thing is to be aware of this and try and live our lives within our own limitations and capabilities. It is so important to be ourselves instead of frequently trying to change who we are so we can fit in with other people's way of doing things. As we allow ourselves to be guided by our own rhythm, life flows in a much more effortless way, so we keep that sense of who we are alive. Unfortunately, it can be hard to do this in our mad crazy world so is it any wonder that we feel out of harmony at times.

So how on earth do we keep ourselves on track? After all we do have responsibilities whether we like it or not so we need all the help we can get. No matter how much we would like to avoid the everyday stresses of day-to-day life it's just not possible. What we have to do though is find ways to deal with whatever life throws at us so that we can keep a sense of inner calm when all around us is going mad. By becoming more aware of the unique natural flow of the seasons we can learn so much about ourselves. Nature is all around us, ready to lavish on us it's wonderful lessons. Showing us that there are times to create and cultivate. Times of rebirth, renewal and new beginnings, times of darkness and quiet for growth and learning. Of course we all have our favourite time of year and our own favourite season but maybe instead of fighting against a particular time we should try instead to live more in harmony with whatever that season has to offer.

I had a lovely conversation with an elderly gentleman who loved nothing better than to reminisce about times gone by. He loved to tell me that us "young ones" hadn't a clue about hardship and we were all just too soft and had everything far too easy. Now there were times when I didn't want to listen to him waffling on but his stories about life without electricity had a certain charm to them. Don't get me wrong when I say that—let me assure you I have no immediate plans to disconnect our electricity. I'm well aware that times gone by had their own hardships to deal with and life was by no means easy for them. What I am saying is that we can learn something from it. You see they had no choice but to live by the seasons. Nature and the natural cycle of day and night controlled their day-to-day life. He described rising early in the summer and working right through the long summer days. Winter on the other hand meant that their working days were shorter. They had to be guided by daylight as all they had were candles and oil lamps. When night-time came work stopped and as darkness set in everything became quiet and still. As the earth settled into this state the mood and atmosphere inside would do likewise. His mother would have the fire lighting and they would gather around it for light and heat. After a long day's work in the fresh air sleep would be effortless deep and satisfying.

A lot can be learned from those times and it has to be said that with all our advances in technology and our mad busy lifestyles we do tend to ignore the natural cycle of the earth. Twilight has now become a time when lights go on and activity continues without pause late into the night. Our senses are bombarded with all sorts of artificial noise so is it any wonder then that we find it difficult to suddenly unwind at bedtime and drift into a natural sleep? We should see winter as a time to slow down, to hibernate, to conserve energy. It is the season with the greatest potential for spiritual growth in preparation for spring and all it's gifts. All nature is at peace, animals hibernate and the earth becomes quiet and bare. As winter darkness and stillness prevails we draw inwards and have time to find our own inner light.

Our awareness of comfort and security is heightened as we sit beside a warm fire or lie in bed listening to the elements of winter howl through the night. The long dark evenings are a time to follow our natural instincts, to dim the lights and relax, to read, to chat or just be alone with our thoughts. When our children were small, they always loved when our electricity would be off. There would be a mad rush for candles and if the fire was lit we would have no choice but to gather there for light and heat. The house would take on a mysterious, shadowy atmosphere and for a while we would create our own entertainment playing cards or some other board game. The novelty would inevitably wear off, especially when their favourite television programme would be due to start but even as children they recognized something magical and satisfying in the silence and darkness. Of course I loved the effect candlelight had on our house. Making everywhere seem lovely in the shadows so that the dirty windows and dusty shelves would fade into oblivion. Maybe I will get the electricity disconnected after all...I really do sometimes think that I should have been born in a different era!

As winter draws to a close, like nature, we feel as though we are awakening from a long sleep. As we awaken, we see tulips, daffodils, snowdrops peep out of the earth. Unseen and silently their roots have established themselves in the earth throughout the long winter in preparation for further growth in spring. So even in the cold emptiness of winter they have been at work. All the earth seems new as greenness pushes through unnoticed and as darkness diminishes we feel a sense of renewal in the newness of it all. Birds sing and the scent of new flowers fills the air. Our hearts are filled with gratitude for this springtime happiness. Night shadows' silently melt away leaving us with a spring in our step as the sun bursts over the horizon bringing long days of light and sunshine.

As summertime approaches our energy levels increase. When the sun is delivering it's lovely warm rays we have the chance to be outdoors, running barefoot in the wonderful lush green earth that nature has created. Schools are closed, routines fall by the wayside as children enjoy their long school break. All of nature seems to shout, telling us to come out and see the beauty that pervades everything. Our senses are heightened to the fragrances of summer—freshly cut grass, a whiff of a barbeque's unique smoky aroma somewhere in the distant garden as evening draws to a close. Sea air, salt water and the sound of the waves all contribute to a growing sense of calm. It is no coincidence that meditators and many religious orders treat the moments before sunrise as the most precious time of the day. God's handwriting is all around us as we walk in places of beauty—in the countryside among trees. We reinforce our connection with the earth by being close to nature. A tree that has withstood the elements for maybe a hundred years or more has a soothing effect on us. It is a silent reminder of the shortness of our lives. As we walk in the woods, our anger dissolves, breathing becomes slower and so our whole body relaxes. These wonderful trees give so much oxygen that we are energized as well as relaxed. With this relaxation our emotions are more in control. All our burdens seem lighter as our body experiences that powerful energy of the earth flowing through every cell and organ. Being amongst nature and all it's beauty makes us absorb everything through our senses. We are subconsciously connecting ourselves to the earth and so are becoming grounded.

When I was happily writing this chapter my eighteen-year-old son Niall was curious to know what I was writing about. When I told him it was about "the seasons" he put his eyes to heaven and said "oh, you're off again with all that hippie stuff." I'm beginning to think that all my family humour me for a quiet life. Really they probably think I'm a bit daft but are too nice to tell me to my face! They certainly can be very cynical about what I say at times but then again, as I said earlier, we are all unique and entitled to our opinion no matter how cynical it is.

Maybe you are feeling the same way. Well then, how about putting it to the test? Go to your favourite place, one you associate with beauty, a wood, a beach, or indeed anywhere in the countryside, if you can't get to the countryside, just sit in your garden. Sit with your feet firmly on the ground and allow your mind to be still. Don't force it; accept the time it takes for your mind to clear and be quiet. Allow yourself to listen; really listen and so become aware of all the sights, sounds, and smells all around you. The feeling that comes over you is the very essence of calm. You are allowing the energy of the earth to enter your body and so become one with all the surrounding beauty. Is it any wonder that people who live in cities are drawn to visit the countryside at weekends? They are following their natural instincts to connect with the healing energy of the earth. This is hard to do in an environment of concrete and tarmacadam where you cannot feel the earth beneath your feet. As my awareness of this grows I find myself more and more exhausted if I spend too long in a city environment. After a day like this I love nothing better than to walk barefoot in my garden. It's as though I have to ground myself each time and touch back into the earth to restore my energy.

Summer passes by, schools reopen; routines in the home become established once more. Mothers find time for themselves after the demands of child filled houses all summer long. Autumn is the time for reaping the harvest and storing it for the winter months, a time of fruition after the growth of summer. As nature slows down everything changes from greens, yellows, reds to a thousand shades of russets and brown. The earth takes on yet another beauty, as falling leaves create their own authentic imprint on the earth. As the daylight hours lessen, we gradually settle into a slower pace allowing ourselves to flow easily into the stillness of winter. These rhythms of nature are God given, natural and free. They weave into each other as sure as night follows day, bringing lessons of hope and realization that each phase of our lives is a natural occurrence. So we should have the courage to be ourselves, to live fully in the world at all times, to find golden moments in the midst of all the madness. Take it as the gift it is and above all be happy.

Wisdom is available from all the people we meet, listening for it can only be done with your own ears.

A Helping Hand

I am Helping Myself when...

1.　　I acknowledge that I am still alive and in control of my body, even though my world seems to be full of previously unknown people making lots of decisions about me. I will not become a passive bystander in my quest for wellness, so I will ask as many questions as I want, no matter how trivial they seem. To remember all these questions, I will keep a notebook with me so I remember them when I visit my doctor.

2.　　To maintain that control I will see my illness not as a failure but as a challenge, an opportunity to explore other therapies that may enhance my conventional treatment and help me cope better with whatever my illness brings. I will find ways that are right for me, and only when I am ready, and, of course with my doctor's consent. I owe it to myself to accept my vulnerability at this time so I will always ensure that whatever therapist I choose is properly trained to deal with me. I certainly will not be pressurised into spending money with people offering me miracle cures.

3.   **I will graciously accept help** as it is offered to me and I will acknowledge that it is not a sign of weakness to say "yes! I need help." People do feel helpless in the face of illness so they need to feel useful, so by saying "yes" I am not only helping them but myself as well. It is okay to let them know how vulnerable I am. They are vulnerable too.

4.   **I stop borrowing trouble from tomorrow,** I take each day as it comes, accepting that we all only have today. Cancer diagnosis or not, we all have an uncertain future. What I imagine may happen is far worse to bear than the reality. It is not how long I live that's important, but what I do with my life. I will constantly find moments to smile and be at peace in the midst of all the madness. I will find enjoyment in the simplest of things.

5.   **I am gentle and kind to myself** by accepting the limitations of my illness instead of constantly fighting against it, wasting valuable energy. I will not be afraid to ask for a hug if I feel sad and alone, and I will hug myself if I can't find anyone to comfort me. I won't waste energy trying to change my life too fast with diets, therapies, etc. Instead I'll learn to deal with whatever I can at any one time. In this gentleness I will truly learn to love and respect who and what I am, warts and all. I will accept that I am only human and there's no need to be "superwoman"!

6.   **I will try to be totally honest** with myself about my thoughts and fears. By acknowledging my sadness, as well as my happiness, I am being true to myself so I can be at peace in my own company. By finding my own inner peace, those around me will feel that peace also. So there will be no need for false smiles and statements like "you're looking great" and "sure I'm grand," when we all know I look like something the cat dragged in! Hopefully that honesty will ripple to those around me so they can be at ease in my pres-

ence. As I acknowledge my sadness I will not lose my capacity for joy and happiness. I will give myself permission to laugh and smile and hold on to my sense of humour because laughter really is food for my soul.

7.   **I will surround myself with people** who allow me the freedom to be honest. People who are at ease with my pain and who know there's more to being positive than an outward public smiling face. People who are able to be totally present with me when my world seems to be falling apart... and don't try to "fix it." It's enough that they are there with me. For those who cannot do this, I cannot carry them as well as myself. They must find their own way to deal with their fears. It's not their fault that they can't carry my pain, and it's not my place to judge.

8.   **I will not feel guilty** about the limitations of my illness or even about getting sick in the first place. Guilt is such a useless waste of energy, so instead of allowing it take me over when I can't do all that I used to, I will acknowledge this time as being difficult knowing and trusting that it will pass. When people try to find reasons for my illness, I will not feel guilty if their questions seem to say I was working too hard, ignoring my body's needs, etc etc. Instead, I will accept myself as I am and know that there isn't always a clear answer to everything as much as I would like to think there is.

9.   **I see my illness as an opportunity in disguise** to explore my spirituality, providing me with time I wouldn't normally have had, to question and explore my role and existence in life. To tap into that unknown space inside myself and see beyond my limitations. To find that inner part of me that has been hidden for so long but has always been there. To ask myself "why me?" and "is this all there is?" To look at, and confront the reality of death and accept it as a part

of life. On this amazing journey I will get to know myself all over again and so realise that as I cherish and draw nearer to my own soul I will learn to trust in it's wisdom and surrender to each new day and what it brings.

10.   **By surrendering each day and accepting that I will be carried,** I will find peace in letting go. This peace will allow me to use my thoughts to make a conscious connection to heal myself. To do this, I will accept the very real power of my thoughts and I will make a daily affirmation of my choice...like, "everyday in everyway I get better and better." I will learn to visualise my body healing—to visualise the healing energy of everyone's prayers and positive thoughts coming towards me. In this constant awareness, I will live every single moment, using every thought I have to heal, to renew and to really and truly "be positive."

Family and Friends You are Helping me when...

1.   **You hold back on giving constant advice,** telling me what you think I should or shouldn't be doing. Instead you allow me time, space and support, so I can find my own way, making my experience a very personal one, even if sometimes you don't always agree and it goes against your way of thinking.

2.   **You don't try to "fix" everything for me,** by saying "you'll be fine" and "sure we all have to die sometime." You can't take my problem from me even though I know you really want to. By trying to "over-do" and "over-fix" everything with a constant cheerleading attitude, you'll end up turning me into a helpless victim, and so you will inevitably end up hating and resenting the burden I'd become. Okay, so I have cancer, but I'm still me, with the same opinions

and feelings. My diagnosis doesn't mean that I've suddenly become a passive shadow of my former self. There's no need to play cheerleading games with me to constantly divert my thoughts away from fear and worry. By doing this you encourage me to ignore my feelings, which makes my worries seem trivial and unimportant.

3.   **You don't expect my illness not to affect you.** Maybe by your "over-doing," "over-fixing" cheerleading attitude you are not really protecting me, but are avoiding your own fears and concerns about cancer. I know you mean well, but how about focussing on your own needs and remember it's okay to be scared, to be sad and even terrified. I am at times, so maybe by sharing these fears you'll allow me to express my feelings too. Everyone is afraid at some stage, no matter how much they say they're not. The more you try to deny it, the harder it gets to keep on smiling. So instead of trying to get rid, or run away from your demons, why not face them instead. We could even do it together.

4.   **You don't overburden me with too many suggestions,** about diets, therapies, self-help books, etc etc. Instead, allow me to take one step at a time. Deal with whatever moment I am in, so I can discover for myself what I need and when I need it and what is best for me. Okay, it may be hard for you to hold back from jumping right in and overloading me with all sorts of ideas. After all, you only want to help. Remember though, I have a lot of stuff to deal with just getting through each day. I'm already on "information overload!" When the time is right I'll ask for help.

5.   **You don't try to convert me to all things "religious,"** especially when I'm not ready. Instead of overloading me with prayers, novena's and relics, why not pray for me instead? At the moment I just don't have the energy and I need to be carried for a while. Why not light a candle in my name

and send me lots of healing positive thoughts. By doing this you are helping me in the greatest way possible.

6. **You don't unintentionally make me feel responsible for my illness** by asking me things like...did you smoke? examine your breasts? work too hard, etc.? I don't need the extra burden of feeling that I have somehow contributed to my illness by not being in tune with my own needs.

7. **You accept me as I am on both the good and bad days,** and are at ease being present when I'm sad and afraid. You are able to just let me be even if I seem to be losing control. You are able to spend time with me—not doing anything but just being at peace in the silence. And remember, it's not your fault if you can't do this. I won't judge you because of it.

8. **You offer loads of practical help,** and you respect my right to refuse that help if I don't want it. If I do accept, well the kind of things that would be most beneficial to me are...school / hospital runs, dinners in the freezer, ironing, general housework...the list is endless and I for one will never refuse!

9. **Finally, if you want to buy me a present** but don't know what to get, let me make some suggestions. Any one of these maybe just what I need to get me started on my own healing journey...

(a) Voucher for a massage or any kind of pampering bodywork therapy;

(b) Tape or CD of nice relaxing music or a voucher for same;

(c) Inspirational books, okay I said not to overburden me with too many suggestions of therapies, self help books, etc. But if you buy me one I can read it at a time that is right for me.

(d) Funny videos or DVDs, because laughter really

is a great medicine and we all need to laugh, no matter how bad things seem.

10.   **Now if you are feeling really generous** and you want to totally spoil me, lots of ideas come to mind…hotel / health spa breaks, sun holidays, luxury cruises. But that would be just too much and I couldn't accept such generosity so I'd have to say no…but then again, I wouldn't want to hurt your feelings, now would I!

What the caterpillar calls the end of the world, the Master calls a butterfly.

Richard Bach

Some of My Best Friends Are Dogs!

IT'S REALLY HARD TO BELIEVE there maybe people who just don't like dogs or indeed any kind of four legged creatures for that matter. Some of you just cannot understand why us dog lovers love our pets so much. It could even be said that you would go so far as to question our sanity, especially when we get very passionate talking about our own little mutts! I can even say that I have been at the receiving end of some rather questioning looks from time to time! Those looks are sure to get even more questioning as until now I have only talked about these great loves of my life (i.e. my two dogs) and here I'm taking things a bit further by writing about them as well. Why, you may ask, am I writing about dogs in a book about breast cancer recovery? Well, indulge me awhile as I explain myself. When I decided to write my recovery story I also decided to write about everything that I feel helped me on the road to that recovery. To put it simply, getting our first dog, Jessie, when I was sick, not only played an important part in my getting well, but also that of my family too. So now I need to explain why I believe this is so. It goes without saying that all you dog lovers out there will instantly understand where I'm coming from. You will know how hard it is to put into words the emotional connection that occurs between a pet and it's owner. To those of you who aren't dog lovers, well all I can say is read on anyway. Who knows, you may even change your mind and your new way of thinking may find you looking at these four legged creatures in a whole new light.

So what is it about us animal lovers that make us love our pets so much? Well, for starters they don't answer back or give cheek. They don't have to be fed at night and no matter what happens their love and devotion is unchanging. Sometimes they smell like musty old boots and leave hairs everywhere. They mistake that lovely green carpet for the garden; even mistake that lovely houseplant as a hiding place for treasured bones and such like. They don't often do a lot or understand that little two letter word "no." In fact, they can be the laziest, dirtiest things in the house. Having said all that, they can be the most loving and loyal companions to us human beings regardless of our age, sex, religion or colour! Our need to be loved is a deep basic part of us all. Being loved is what nurtures us and makes us who we are. We experience that love from many different sources— parents, children, siblings, friends, and partners. Sometimes however, things change. Children grow up and leave home, parents may separate or die, friends move on and generally life brings many detours and unavoidable changes that influence everything about us and our way of thinking.

It's a well-known fact that caring for a pet does lower stress levels, reduce blood pressure and generally creates feelings of calm and relaxation. I worked in two different nursing homes where the owners were dog lovers and so their pets were very much a part of daily life for the elderly residents. Certainly, without a shadow of doubt, their presence was a great source of pleasure to all of them. Clinical evidence shows that where Alzheimer's patients have access to caring for pets, i.e. brushing, feeding, walking, etc., their attention span improves and so they are generally more relaxed and content. It has been proven that children who grow up with a family pet develop greater empathy and kindness towards others. I suppose then you could say that no matter what the age is, pets lessen the feelings of loneliness and isolation and so increase our self-esteem. Just the simple exercise of stroking a pet has a marked effect on our mood—even slowing down our heart rate and lowering our blood pressure...providing that it's not a vicious Rottweiler of course!!

Earlier, in part one, I spoke about how Jessie and then Bonzo came into our lives, so I won't repeat myself all over again. I will say though, all the clinical evidence I just spoke about didn't influence us. It was more a feeling that it was what we all needed at such a difficult time in our lives. I also spoke in Part One about my father's great love of animals, and of his wonderful affinity and understanding of them. His beloved Judy was his constant companion. Such was her devotion to him that when he died, she pined so much that she died shortly afterwards. He had a strong connection with animals and I have no doubt that he played a big part in awakening that connection and love of animals in me and my family. He knew exactly what we all needed at such a low point in our lives. He knew how much light and happiness a dog would bring to our home. As I have said over and over again, our loved ones who died are constantly caring and watching over us. We only have to trust in that knowledge and awareness for good things to happen. Over the years our children often asked about getting a family pet but we always found reasons not to. When I was nearing the end of my chemotherapy our daughter Mary asked about getting a dog for Christmas and it just felt like a very good idea at the time. Once the decision was made it seemed like the most natural thing in the world and getting Jessie was very easy. Likewise, when we considered getting a second dog a few years later, it happened just as effortlessly and so Bonzo came to stay. I do, however draw the line at two. I'm not going to even think about getting another one in case one suddenly appears out of nowhere on our doorstep!

And so Jessie, a Yorkshire terrier, came to live with us on Christmas Eve, sporting a big red bow and bringing with her lots of excitement and laughter. We had all been through a difficult few months and her arrival certainly lightened all our moods. Suddenly she was there to be cared for, to be fed watered and walked. So no matter how full of self-pity any of us were, we still had to do all these things. We had to think about someone else besides ourselves, which was really a good thing, as it helped to motivate us and just get on with things. Doing these simple tasks soon became a pleasure, as we would be showered with so much affection and love, which was endearing and heart-warming. Having so much loyalty and love directed towards us, even from an animal, can only bring to the surface all that is good in us. So those feelings of kindness, empathy and caring increase our "feel good" factor. Our children soon became very attached to Jessie and it can only be good to see them being kind towards her and caring for her in such a loving way. Mind you, they aren't always the first to volunteer when she needs walking or feeding. At those times they can all suddenly become very busy!

As I was the person most often at home she soon became my constant shadow. On my "off" days she would just sit looking at me as if sensing my sadness. She would usually lie beside me in bed or sit on my lap, always watchful. Her constant silent presence seemed to have an effect on me and I frequently found myself crying copious tears and telling her all my deep sad thoughts. It was as though her presence allowed me the freedom to be myself and express my feelings, knowing she couldn't say or do anything but absorb my sadness. Some days I did question my sanity...after all I was talking to an animal! At the time it felt like the most natural thing in the world to do. No matter what my mood was her attitude towards me never changed. That unchanging attitude and unconditional love is at the heart of why we love our pets so much. She remains a constant pleasure in our home and manages to bring out the best in all of us. It is so easy to see why anyone who lives alone can benefit from having a pet. Sometimes people living alone will say they have no reason to get up in the mornings. Having a dog to feed and care for motivates them to get up and so lessens their feelings of isolation and depression.

We now have two dogs, Bonzo, a Jack Russell, came to live with us about two years after Jessie. He never fails to bring a smile to everyone's face, as due to a head injury he continuously goes around in circles. Some will even say that he suit's our family very well because of this! I wonder whatever do they mean? I still find myself talking to both of them and I no longer question my sanity about it. You see, family pets become like a natural extension of the family unit, so it's not uncommon to hear any one of our family talking to them without even realising that they're doing so. It's also not uncommon to hear torrents of abuse being directed at one of them, especially when they find their way into something or somewhere they shouldn't be. . like the bin for example. They really are worth all the extra responsibility, as our home never feels empty. They welcome us at the door every time as if they have never seen us before, going mad with excitement and wagging tails. We never feel alone even if we are the only person in the house, so increasing our feelings of security. Okay, there is work and responsibility involved and I do sometimes question the expression "man's best friend," as sometimes it's the woman doing all the caring! It's a small price to pay. There's more to caring than just the physical things. They love to be spoilt, to be loved and to get loads of attention. I can honestly tell you that by doing so we get back such undying devotion and adoration that we can only ever imagine getting from any human being.

I can say now that it would be hard to ever imagine our home without a family pet. It would certainly seem a lot emptier, quieter and possibly cleaner, of course. Maybe if I had never got sick we would have continued to find reasons not to have a family pet. My illness certainly acted as the catalyst in doing so, and so we have all gained so much. I believe that animals have their own unique innate healing qualities that affect us on many levels. They really do form a spiritual connection with us human beings. Because they can't talk they communicate through instinct so encouraging us to do the same. So the communication is more on a spiritual level. We all have our own natural instincts but because we talk so much we don't always use, or tap into it. Animals do heighten our awareness of this, which of course explains the wonderful effect they have on us. Our daughter Mary summed up my feelings very well in 2002. She filled out an application form nominating Jessie for "Pet of the Year" competition. One of the questions asked was "why do you believe your dog should win this award?." Mary replied, "because Jessie made my mum smile when she had cancer." She said it all in that one sentence. Jessie didn't win, but she did come second and both herself and Bonzo continue to make me smile every day.

For they fail to understand the other who have not heard themselves, and they are blind to the reality of others who have not probed themselves. The perfect listener hears you even when you say nothing.

Anthony de Mello

Counselling, It's Good to Talk

I FEEL VERY LUCKY to have survived the whole cancer experience without "cracking up." Now there are some who might say I'm a bit daft anyway, but I'm happy with my "daftness" and that's all that matters as far as I'm concerned. I do like to think that I'm fairly well grounded. I also feel very lucky that I live every day to the full and as worry free as is possible in this mad, crazy world of ours. When I was first diagnosed, I thought I'd never know a day's peace again, so I feel I have come a long way since that time. Getting to this point has involved a lot of soul searching and up and downs. I've worked hard at maintaining a peaceful mind and continue to do so each day by having a constant awareness of my thoughts and feelings.

I believe that living with a cancer diagnosis we have to work that extra bit harder to be positive and in control. Okay, we must acknowledge all our emotions that go with it, but we can't afford to let too much negativity or dark thoughts take over. When someone says to me "you're so positive and are looking great," I like to remind him or her that I'm not always smiling. It doesn't just happen and it does take some commitment and work on my part. Now I'm surely not trying to act the martyr or look for a clap on the back. It's just that sometimes people only see what they want to believe and think "well she looks okay so it mustn't be too bad." I'm not passing judgement about them but it's just the way it is. Sometimes they can't face the reality of cancer and all that goes with it so they choose to ignore it and that's okay too, after all that is their way. However, they can then go on to tell the newly diagnosed person about Mary or Maggie who "are in great form altogether" and have had breast cancer. The newly diagnosed person may then think, "well I better smile if Mary or Maggie can." The reality being that behind that smile they are tormented and afraid while putting on the right face for others. You see, Mary or Maggie had probably gone through a lot of emotions to be able to reach that stage of really smiling. That's why I feel a certain responsibility to explain myself and where I'm coming from. I'm sure a lot of the time they are sorry to have said anything at all! I am inclined to go on a bit, aren't I?

Now, please don't get me wrong. I loved, and still do, to hear success stories. In fact I could say that for a long time I latched on to these stories as a source of hope and inspiration. On the down side though, were the not so lucky stories of people who hadn't survived, that I couldn't run away from or deny. So other people's stories gave me great hope on one hand but incredible sadness on the other. The fear would be all consuming and terrifying and I'd have to really work hard at getting myself back on track. In fact no matter how many stories we hear, either good or bad, it's not our story. We have to deal with our own cancer, our fears, worries, up's and downs. Our journey is ours alone. Be influenced and helped by so many people but we cannot live our lives through them continuously and so we must find our own unique and very personal way. Yes! be inspired by others but it's not good to constantly follow another human being. Every person must look at their own self, listen to their own inner guide and realise that actually their best teacher is within themselves and not in those around them. Being told that it could be worse is no help either because even if someone else has an apparently greater crisis in their lives, you still have to close your own eyes and deal with your own thoughts in your own way. Being told that someone else is worse off, is denying you the right to acknowledge and feel your own pain, even making you feel guilty about feeling sad and do you know what—it's okay to feel like shit!

We all practice denial everyday of our lives. We hide bills hoping they'll go away if we don't look at them. We avoid looking in the mirror if we are feeling fat and unattractive. The same can happen when we are faced with a bigger crisis of any sort. We may try to continue as if nothing has happened. We'll do everything we can to keep busy, anything at all that stops us from looking at ourselves and questioning "why me?" Whether we like it or not, everything that happens to us either good or bad stays with us. It's there in our psyche and makes us who we are. Every experience is what we make it and every problem we face has a purpose; it can be an opportunity to educate or inspire us, creating a chance to learn more about ourselves. We would like to think that our lives would remain problem free but really these problems are an opportunity for spiritual growth if we have the courage to deal with them head on. We are only human though, so how we choose to do that is up to us and there are no rules or timetables involved. Sometimes then, other people's fighting talk can drive us insane; even make us feel inadequate, especially when we are struggling to cope. Talk of putting up a fight has undertones of doing ten rounds with Mike Tyson as far as I'm concerned and it's not an image I want to associate with my life.

Following a crisis of any sort, often the last thing one needs is to be told to go for counselling. Sometimes we just need to unravel our thoughts and come to terms with what is happening to us. We may not be ready to bare our soul to a total stranger. We may not want to let our guard down in case that, once we start we won't be able to get up and go again. We can be afraid of where it will take us—that we will be judged by the person listening and of course sometimes we just don't allow ourselves time. Unfortunately, we do put up a front a lot of the time that covers up our real feelings. We come into the world as pure uncomplicated beings. Over the years, however, that purity becomes masked by years of accumulated baggage. The purity gets totally lost and our artificial face is what we believe to be who we really are. It is our way of surviving, but over time it becomes harder to keep up that front. The danger then is that our suppressed feelings build up inside and we can have a tendency to "leak" all over the place. By this I mean off-loading to anyone who happens to be there when we are feeling under pressure to talk. Unfortunately, that particular person may not always be as discreet as we would like, it just happened they were there when we needed an ear. This can leave us feeling even more exposed and fragile. This is where counselling is so beneficial. We can off-load our fears in a safe and secure environment knowing that whatever we say won't go any further.

I felt very fragile and vulnerable for a long time and so I was afraid to bare my soul in case I'd get hurt even more. The idea of going for counselling was the last thing I wanted to do. I was quite happy to write my thoughts down on paper, safe in the knowledge that no one could see it, only me. I had no set routine about this, just whenever I felt the need to get something off my chest. It was great, because even though my family were very supportive we were all inclined to protect each other by not saying out loud our worst fears. I needed to be able to acknowledge the fact that I might die, but I also knew how much I would upset everyone by saying this. So writing down all this was a great starting point for me. I never read back what I wrote and eventually I burned the whole thing along with my wig, which was great fun, I might add!

When I did decide to go for counselling it was about three years after my diagnosis and the time felt right for me. I believe that the time has to be right and only you will know when. Counselling isn't for everybody but if there are questions and feelings going around in your head that just won't go away well then it's a good place to start. You see, it's not about anyone else's thoughts and feelings just your own. Our eldest son, Eoin, had started college and it seemed to spark a huge rush of emotions in me that I knew I had to deal with. I was ready to trust someone else with my thoughts and I was also curious to see where it would take me. There was a free service available in our area called "The Wexford Cancer Counselling Service." I made an appointment to see Freda Hanley who was the trained counsellor attached to the service. As she was a trained nurse and psychotherapist I felt I was putting myself in safe hands. When you are feeling raw and vulnerable you are terrified that someone will say something that hurts you even more. I believe strongly that we owe it to ourselves when we decide to go to a therapist, that we are sure of their qualifications. In the whole area of holistic therapy/complimentary medicine there are so many people working who really aren't properly trained or qualified. Sadly they can cause so much unnecessary pain due to their lack of knowledge and experience. A well-trained therapist should always respect where the client is in his or her life, and then only take them as far as they are able to go. The responsibility does lie with ourselves though, as to whom we choose to go to, but unfortunately when we are vulnerable we can be misguided leading to even more confusion and stress for ourselves.

Deciding to go for counselling and making the first appointment can be the hardest part. That decision can raise so many fears that you may want to back out before you even start. Mainly for me it was the fear of the unknown, of digging too deep and discovering something sinister about myself that I had blocked out for years. Also, a feeling of being "self" indulgent, talking about no one but myself. But you see it's not about anyone else but yourself. Every human being is of equal importance, has work to do in this world and has equal potential. How we perceive ourselves and how much we are willing to look at and change ourselves decides how we interact with people and how they see us. We all have free will as to whether we want to make changes and so continue to grow and develop spiritually. We can after all only change ourselves, by doing so we can inspire others to look at themselves and change too. Life is like a mirror; smile and it will smile back at you. If we love people enough they will respond lovingly back. If we offend and hurt others we will be offended and hurt back. When we approach someone in judgement they will become defensive. Whereas if we approach them with love and compassion they will look at themselves instead of those around them. So it all starts with ourselves no matter now much we like to blame everyone else for our problems. I really hadn't a clue what to expect when I decided to go for counselling. I knew it would involve me doing a lot of talking and Freda doing a lot of listening. How long each session would last or indeed how many sessions I would need to go for were the issues I was vague about. For me personally, each session lasted for about an hour and I went for six or eight sessions over a few months. No two people are the same though, so everyone's own experience will be uniquely theirs. An experience that will be deeply personal and relevant to no one else but themselves.

I developed a pretty instant trust in Freda. I soon realised that I could say anything and just be myself in that room, knowing that she wasn't going to advise or comment, just listen. We can have a mistaken consideration for others in choosing to bare our burden alone, so it was great to be able to talk, knowing I wasn't hurting or upsetting anyone. The more I talked the deeper I seemed to reach down into my soul. A lot of our talk is just superficial chitchat. When I got that out of the way I felt I was really digging deep and stirring the pot of my emotions, and the more I talked the lighter I felt. I scratched away at the surface and found that uncomplicated child I once was. It was exhausting but so very worthwhile, making me stronger and more understanding of myself.

At some stage along the way I had a dream that for me seemed so very significant at the time, as I was working my way through many emotions and long forgotten memories. In the dream I was trying to climb up a hill that had what appeared to be farmyard slurry pouring down it. I was also carrying a baby, to which I had absolutely no emotional attachment. It seemed to be such a burden, holding me back and slowing me down. Now I'm certainly not a dream interpreter or anything but I do believe it signified for me a letting go of a lot of "shit" (excuse the language!) that I had accumulated and unknowingly held on to over the years.

By talking it out of my system it was as though I was climbing out of the "shit" and the baby was the burden of carrying around unnecessary baggage from times throughout my childhood. The baby really was myself.

Thankfully I didn't find anything too sinister as I had feared, just a lifetime of experiences, good and bad, that I was able to look at and accept as part of me. I learned to love and accept myself and no longer feel the need to be constantly giving until there was nothing left. Giving for all the wrong reasons—to feed my ego and enhance my self-esteem, to be told how great I was and to be accepted and liked. Now I was doing this without even realising it and so by learning to like, even love myself, I no longer feel the need to look beyond myself for fulfilment. Because of this awareness I now give because I want to so it is really from the heart. Finding that uncomplicated child again has made me see the great freedom in simplicity. The more possessions that we try to accumulate the more they control and become a burden to us. Our possessions go on to possess us when we allow them to. Now don't get me wrong, I still like my comfort and I won't refuse the lotto, if I win it, but my basic needs are simple ones. I feel when I have health, happiness and a peaceful mind that I am richer than rich. One day Freda explained to me that psychotherapy means, "soul healing." I never knew that, but I can now understand why. I feel that going for counselling played a very big part in helping me to heal my soul. By allowing myself to be gently led by Freda, as far as I wanted to go, I learned to trust my own soul. By trusting in her gentleness I came to realise that as I grow and change there is no need to be afraid. Instead of everything being strange and new, it is all reassuringly familiar and safe because it's simply a journey back to that uncomplicated child I once was.

The world is round and the place which may seem like the end may also be only the beginning.

Ivy Barker Priest

The Circle of Life

SOMEONE ONCE SAID TO ME that we are all dying from the moment we are born and they are possibly right. We certainly can't deny that we will all die sometime, no matter how much we try to run away, or hide from that reality. After all, we can't have birth without death and we can't talk about dying without talking about living. Whether we like it or not, in the years ahead, be it ten, twenty or eighty, most of us will have died. This thought is without doubt a sobering one and doesn't leave much room for inflated egos or pride. You probably think I'm very morbid but really I'm just stating a reality—a reality that is certainly heightened by a serious illness such as cancer. It does become that bit harder to deny the possibility of death following such a diagnosis. After all it's staring us in the face—our greatest fear is right there in front of us and there's nowhere to run. We may try to run—to deny it but it will still be there, no matter what we try to do. Maybe then we should let that fear motivate us to examine our existence and true value in life. Instead of becoming obsessed with dying and when it will happen, we will then blossom and grow. Learning to appreciate the wonderful gift of life and be at peace in the knowing that we will all die sometime. Facing the fact that you have come close to death is one of life's greatest levellers. People who have had near death experiences will often say that death no longer holds any fear over them such was the nature of the feeling of peace and serenity that they experienced—a feeling of never being alone. Most will say that they themselves decided to return to the physical world to continue their learning even though it was so beautiful and free where they went.

The reality of knowing and accepting that we all have to die sometime helps us to gain a whole new perspective on life. It helps us to let go of a lot of the nonsense that can take us over and instead focus on what is important to us on our precious journey through life. If we were to ask ourselves, "if this was the last day of our lives, how would I want to live it?" For each of us that question should show us what it is that makes us truly happy and content. Maybe then we should approach each day as if it were our last, and then no matter whether we are healthy or sick, our quality of life will become increasingly richer. I do need to emphasise that I do not have a death wish. I love life and want to go on living for as long as I can. However, by accepting the reality of death as part of our lives we are given the opportunity to learn our greatest lessons about living. I know for certain what my answer to that question would be. I certainly wouldn't want to waste a minute of it cleaning, shopping, accumulating, or making endless "to do" lists. I'd just want to be with those I love (dogs included) nowhere exotic now! Feeling at peace in the knowing that I had experienced both the giving and receiving of love, and knowing too that our wonderful gift of love for each other will go on even beyond death. Love, tenderness, kindness and friendship are truly life's greatest gifts and can never be substituted by any amount of material things, no matter how much we try to accumulate or possess them.

We come into this life with many lessons to be learned. Our soul is our constant guide and protector but we must get to know and trust it. Doing this is not about staying on the surface of life's experiences, or looking at everything and everyone else as the cause of all our problems. It's about facing life head on and solving our own problems and difficulties. Learning from them…always looking inwards for solutions and answers to these problems. It's about delving beneath the surface, discovering new experiences every moment. Constantly asking, and knowing the answers will always be found within ourselves. It's about letting go of negative thoughts and feelings so in that freedom and trusting we will be guided in a way that is right for us. We all have free will and even though our soul is our inner guide, we are all responsible for our actions and reactions. We can choose how much or how little we want to learn and listen to. But we owe it to ourselves to care for our body, to treat it with respect and to be "self" aware at all times.

Our body is our home, and also the home of our soul. As our soul becomes our guide we will instinctively know what is right or wrong, good or evil. By denying that knowledge, or going against it, we are hurting ourselves again and again. Every problem that comes our way gives us a chance to constantly learn. Whatever lessons we don't learn in this life our soul will go on to the next life with those lessons still to be learned. Heaven and hell are states of being that we can all experience on either side of life. Heaven being when we live in harmony with God and ourselves. By doing so we achieve inner peace, which creates peace all around us. We can then be truly alone with our thoughts and ourselves and not be afraid. Hell on the other hand is the very opposite, when we go against God and ourselves. By creating this constant struggle within ourselves we create our own hell on earth and our thoughts can be our greatest torment. And, of course, when we are tormented it obviously affects all those around us. Once we accept this awareness we can never deny it ever again. It is what separates good and evil for us. We may allow our free will to take us off course every now and then. By allowing that to continue we create our own disharmony, especially when we knowingly do it over and over again. In other words a sin is really a sin when we do something that "the little voice" inside our head is telling us is wrong. A lot of the time we unknowingly do wrong or hurt others, but just haven't woken up to the consequences of our actions yet.

We all grow spiritually at our own pace. The fact that we do is inevitable and not a matter of "if," but of "when." That's why we are here. From the moment of birth we are all developing physically and of course spiritually as well. Each stage of our lives is a new and exciting experience. We accumulate much wisdom along the way and our lifelong search for meaning gives us many opportunities to learn from people we meet and situations we find ourselves in. Again, we all have free will and choice so it's up to us how much or how little we want to learn. All our learning helps us on our journey throughout life. As the years pass we are slowly getting older but life becomes more meaningful from all that we have absorbed and experienced along the way. This ageing process is the most natural thing in the world. As we learn to accept the natural cycle of life we grow old gracefully. We shouldn't feel sadness at our fading beauty and lost youthfulness. We shouldn't try to fight the natural ageing process by resorting to numerous sessions with plastic surgeons—trying to maintain and be identified by our youthful external appearance as a means of happiness. A happiness that stays beyond our reach, if we refuse to connect with the timeless life and beauty within ourselves. This connection makes us, feel at peace in the acceptance of life's natural cycle. How we perceive an experience at twenty or seventy will obviously be totally different so we should always acknowledge the wonderful wisdom of the elderly. They have so much to teach us from a lifetime of experiences. Native American tribes allow grandfathers and grandmothers make important decisions for their community. We should follow their example and be respectful of our ageing population. If we are respectful of the elderly we will bring that self-respect to our own later years when that time comes, because in this circle of life what we give out to others we do receive back.

Our journey ultimately ends with death. By this I mean the process where our physical body dies and returns to the earth but our soul lives on and on. If we view death not as much as a physical process but a spiritual one, we lose a lot of the fear attached to it. In the circle of life isn't it fair to say that birth and death are very similar? I mean the process of the birth into the physical world of new life, and at death the birth of our soul into it's spiritual home. I had the privilege of working as a midwife and so I was present many times as new life came into being. I also had the privilege of caring for and being with many people as they died. At birth the mother struggles with her labour pains and her breathing is erratic and varying as she eventually pushes a usually protesting infant into the world—protesting as though it didn't want to leave it's mother's womb—it's safe cocoon. Death on the other hand sees the person struggling as his or her soul readies it'self for departure from it's home—the physical body. Breathing becomes laboured and noisy and eventually silent and still as the soul passes over and the body becomes cold and empty, eventually returning to the earth. I consider it a real privilege to have been present many times for both these experiences. It has to be the greatest gift to have helped new life into the world and to have helped someone die with dignity and peace.

I haven't always been so philosophical about life and death. I have to be honest and say that as a young carefree student nurse a lot of the spiritual aspect of these experiences went right over my head. When we are at that stage of our lives we are too busy just having fun and certainly are neither interested nor ready to scratch the surface too much. My cancer diagnosis certainly made me confront and become aware of my mortality and I now believe that it takes more courage to live than to die. Some people's lives can involve so much struggle that it really does take courage to get through any one day. Struggles that may be caused by physical or mental illness, indeed a host of reasons that can lead to on-going stress, worry and inner turmoil. Reasons that can make getting out of bed to face a new day a huge effort. Is it any wonder then that it does take a lot of courage to live? But, when we choose to learn more about death we actually learn more about life and how to live it. This may help us to make our daily struggle that bit easier to endure.

My first experience with death was when I was seven. My sister Mary died aged seventeen. She died rather suddenly even though she had a congenital heart disease since birth. My memory of that time has always been a series of frozen images as seen through the eyes of the seven-year-old child I was. Memories of standing at the end of her hospital bed peeping through the bars at her slightly opened eyes, and being totally bewildered as to why everyone was so upset, as

I thought she was just sleeping. Memories of being taken to her coffin to say goodbye and recoiling from the cold marble like quality of her cheek as I touched it. Memories that stayed with me down through the years. Images that never changed, always remaining in that childlike innocent detached way. I thought that being so young it hadn't had a big impact on my life. When I went for counselling, after I got sick, the emotion that seemed to have always been missing from those memories became very real. By talking about, and experiencing those feelings, I revisited that time all over again. This helped me to reach a deeper level of understanding about myself and the effect Mary's death had on myself and my family at the time. Mary's memory has always been a big part of our lives and our daughter is privileged to share her name, a decision that I know meant so much to my mother. Her love lives on in us all and by no means ended with her death.

When we see beyond the physical death and view it spiritually we know that our loved ones are all around us and their love certainly doesn't stop with the death of the physical body. I have absolutely no doubt in my mind in that belief. This was reinforced for me throughout my illness with the feeling of being constantly cared for and protected. My dream about Mary when I was in hospital (which I talk about at the beginning of this book) has remained a constant source of comfort for me. When someone dies we can't see him or her anymore but their very essence remains present in their home. It penetrates every room in the house. You only have to walk into the home of someone who has died and where there has been great love, you can still feel that love everywhere. We have all experienced these feelings when we have visited such homes, often coming away with sadness but a certain feeling of peace as well. Unfortunately, where there has been a lot of unresolved anger or pain this too can linger in the atmosphere long after the person has died. A home is by no means just a combination of bricks and mortar. From my experience, working as a community nurse brought me into many homes where people were being cared for. It didn't matter whether it was a humble cottage or a luxurious house; the atmosphere ultimately is what makes it. The big expensive house with all it's luxury may be a cold unfeeling place to be, while the unassuming simple cottage may be the place where love and the feeling of "home" is very strong. The atmosphere of course being made up of the every essence of those who have lived there. We all experience this every day. Personally speaking, as a mother, I can say that each of my children's bedrooms are easily identifiable as theirs. . not by any one thing but a combination of aspects of themselves that come together to make up their own unique space.

Over the years working in hospitals, we learned to accept death as part of our routine and so dealt with it as best we could. When I was a student nurse it did take time getting used to watching people die. Having then to "lay out" the body was an even bigger, more daunting experience for an eighteen to nineteen year old. It did take time to get used to it and I certainly wasn't thinking too many spiritual and meaningful thoughts. I was usually more focussed on getting the job done and most definitely trying to avoid being left alone with the body. If there was something needed I was always first to volunteer to go for it. If I did find myself alone for any length of time my imagination would run wild thinking I could see the body moving—even breathing. I'd stand as close to the door as possible waiting for whoever was with me to return and then act all cool and calm as if there wasn't a bother on me! As students we would have to accompany the hospital porter as he brought the body to the mortuary. The hospital where I trained was spread out over a large area; this was something none of us liked too much, especially on night duty when everywhere took on an even more eerie atmosphere. The situation we found ourselves in was so surreal that we often found ourselves reacting in the very opposite way to how we were feeling. Instead of being grave and serious we often found ourselves laughing over something totally silly, so relieving the strain. This was by no means disrespectful but when faced with something so great at such a young age, where we were totally out of our depth, the only thing to do was to laugh, often with a certain hysteria attached, I might add.

In latter years I worked as a community nurse which involved many duties, one being caring for the terminally ill in their own homes. While a hospital environment cannot help but have a clinical element attached, caring for someone in his or her own home is a totally different experience. It's no surprise then that people want so much to be at home in their own surroundings and are then able to feel still somewhat in control. It's their home so they feel in charge. Being in hospital, that feeling can be lost in the necessary routine and protocol of hospital life. Unfortunately, family circumstances don't always allow for the person to be at home but thankfully hospice services are becoming more common. Someone once said to me, "it must be awful to be with someone who is doing to die." The initial reaction would be to day "yes," but you see death is by no means a failure. Sometimes everyone can't be cured and when that happens we owe it to that person to make and provide a sensitive caring and peaceful environment as they spend their last days, weeks or months on earth. It is a privilege to be there, and if we could think of it as a process of physical change that is inevitable we stop trying to turn away from it and face it directly with acceptance. Like nature we also go through many cycles. From conception, pregnancy, birth, childhood, adolescence, old age and eventually death. We could possibly ask ourselves on that cycle where does it all begin? Where does it all end? I can't ever remember a time when I didn't exist...can you?

In the home where someone is dying, I have seen so many scenarios unfold. Tensions may come to the surface as families may be forced together over a long period of time. Suddenly life seems to be on hold waiting for the inevitable passing of a loved one. This time can also prove to be one of healing on many levels as unresolved issues are talked about and are dealt with. Memories of happy times are shared reminding everyone of events and moments in their life which can give them an appreciation of all that has been good within their family. The person dying may have so many things he wants to say that loved ones need to hear. Things he has wanted to say but could never find the right moment, words that a son or daughter, sister or brother desperately needs to hear. Words as simple as "I love you," that have never been said before. The person dying may also need to hear those same words, or to hear something that means he or she can be at peace. There can be so much love and reconciliation within a family at this time leading to a feeling of serenity for all concerned, even in the midst of all the sadness. In the acceptance of the inevitability of death, the struggle stops and so there can be great peace. There is a dignity in that acceptance of the inevitable that is truly beautiful .The person dying, stops struggling and instead uses his or her time to say their goodbye's. To make their wishes for their funeral heard and just be in the presence of those they love, savouring every last moment of their precious time. Unfortunately, it doesn't always happen that way. People may not always get a chance to say goodbye due to the suddenness of their parting. They may die alone with no loved ones around them. They may die leaving many issues unresolved. All of which can make the grieving process even harder. We can only hope and pray that on some level they find peace.

The home where someone is dying doesn't have to be all sadness and tears. Often there can be a lot of laughter as stories are shared and memories are recalled. The nicest thing I ever experienced in that situation was spending a night caring for a gentleman who was obviously in his last hours. Instead of tiptoeing around the room and whispering quietly, his wife, family and some friends gathered around the bed and shared many stories about their life down through the years. There was much laughter and tears throughout the night and I have no doubt that the gentleman who was dying took many of those memories with him on his final journey. Instead of creating a stilted, abnormal atmosphere it is better to trust our own natural instincts and be as normal as possible. Where there are no words to be found often it's enough to be totally present with that person so reassuring them that they are not alone. To sit or lie beside them holding their hand we are following our natural instinct to use the wonderful gift of touch to convey our love when words cannot be said. Even if a person is deeply unconscious they can still be comforted by the presence of loved ones around them. Often there is no need to "do" anything and it's enough to just "be."

For the loved ones death is so very final. The emptiness and loneliness can be overwhelming, even more so if the death has been very sudden and unexpected. There is a comfort to be gained from ritual of the wake, funeral, burial and subsequent callers to the house. It is all part of the natural process of saying goodbye. The funeral is a farewell where family and friends recall the good that person has done, reading favourite poems or singing favourite hymns. Those who are grieving are carried along on a wave of loving energy and support as everyone gathers to say their goodbye's. Grieving has no timetable, no rules. Everyone finds their own way. Getting back to normal is good but the pain of loss must be acknowledged and felt. Trying to make life too normal can deny that grief.

When I was a child, grieving widows wore black for the first year following the death of their husbands. By doing so they were allowed to grieve and that process was accepted and acknowledged by society. It wasn't glossed over or pushed aside but openly included in the day-to-day life of everyone. Just because the person is no longer visible doesn't mean that they are no longer present. They live on in all those they have loved. Of course, they should be remembered and talked about freely and openly. They are only a thought away at any one time. I only have to think of my mother and by doing so I get a sense of her presence all around me. We should think of them with love and our prayer for them should be one of peace and in the acceptance of their death we will be able to let go and they will truly be at peace.

In my writing about death I have found myself really writing about life. I've shared some of my thoughts and walked some of the steps of my journey with you. I'm sure that you have already taken some of the same steps and have had some of the same thoughts, but just haven't realised it yet. We are, after all, on a journey and we are all learning right up to the day we die. If we could only realise that, and trust our own natural instincts more by being confident in our own self-knowledge. If we could only accept how short our time on earth is we would be less troubled about dying and more focussed on living. We would be happy when we have enough but not too much. We would know that the best medicine for all our ailments is love—love of ourselves and of those around us. We would come to realise that even if we have nothing we can have everything, even if we are sad we can still smile and be happy. If our mind's focus is continuously on earthly things in our search for happiness it remains elusive and so the earth gains nothing. If, however, we focus on the spiritual aspect of our lives to achieve peace, we become more respectful of ourselves and others and of the universe all around us. We become more appreciative and knowledgeable about what is good and bad and so the earth gains plenty. So the next time you say "don't ask her anything her head is in the clouds."...think again.

People get so in to the habit of worry that if you save them from drowning and put them on the bank to dry in the sun with hot chocolate and muffins, they would worry about catching a cold.

John Jay Chapman

Don't Be Afraid to Be Afraid

June 9th 2005
Waterford Regional Hospital,
Waiting for a bone scan
Conversation with myself.

NERVOUS AND TENSE...*all the old familiar fears are back with a vengeance, all the "what if's" and the "maybe's." Five years since my diagnosis, a significant milestone for me on this journey that is mine, even more significant if I'm still 'all clear' five years on from a diagnosis that I thought was a death sentence. Now this is as real as it gets, there's no room for silly talk here. This machine can see right through me and will be able to relate one of two possible results, positive or negative. I wonder how long will I have to wait for these results...I wonder will it be good or bad news...what then...what if? God why did I bother telling my doctor about that shoulder pain, I should have just ignored it. I'm driving myself mad...they said it would take the radioactive dye two hours to be absorbed* into my bones but it feels like an eternity. The sun is shining so I might as well go outside and be miserable there. Lots of people coming and going, all sorts of expressions, happy, sad, worried, all in their own world with their own concerns. Maybe I'll do the crossword, can't concentrate. For God sake why am I so restless, thought I'd learned everything over the past few years...the power of now/ living the moment and all that kind of thing. Whatever will I do for the next hour? Maybe I'll write, well it has helped me in the past and I am trying to write a book after all. Scribble, scribble, scribble...feeling a bit better, it's helping me to concentrate, to focus, to remember, to remind myself that "yes," I have learned something. It's amazing what happens when I start writing, what I sometimes can't clearly express even to myself is so much easier to write on paper and when I see the words in print it helps me to remember, to recall all sorts of things, to realise that I really do hate waiting in hospitals. In fact I don't want to see my life in terms of waiting, waiting for results, doctor's appointments etc. It's so pointless waiting for things that might not happen. Life is so fragile that if I don't seize the moments they will pass me by and in the blink of an eye they could be gone forever so it would have all been a waste of time.

Time for my scan; gosh time flies when I'm having fun! I do what I am told and lie perfectly still on the table. Lots of hospital staff coming and going, don't feel like talking to strangers, I'll put all my meditation skills into practise. Feeling more and more removed from everybody as I go into my own private space. Scan finished and feeling nice and relaxed. Mobile rings...it's Michael and our daughter Mary "are you ready yet because we're starving and waiting for you to have lunch with us." "Yes," I reply, "I'm on *my way," and off I go into the sunshine in anticipation of having a nice afternoon and do you know what tomorrow and all that goes with it can take care of it'self.*

I believe that if we become acquainted with our fears they lose their power over us and so our fear diminishes. I hope by reading this chapter you too will become acquainted with at least some of your fears and live in a more relaxed and worry free existence. Getting cancer had a very deep and lasting impact on my way of thinking. It radically and dramatically distinguished the past, the present, and the future for me, and by doing so it brought me very definitely into the present. It defined the present time for me like no other experience could; it was as though I faced my worst fears so nothing else could ever be as bad or affect me as much. Initially I drove myself mad with all the "if's" and the "buts," the wonderings and the maybe's. At some stage along the way I realised what a lot of precious time I was wasting. I was, for a while so busy wondering if I'd be around in two, five, possibly ten years, that I was losing valuable time which could have been put to better use enjoying myself.

Having finished my chemo, physically I was recovering well so it was only my own fears and worries that were stopping me from living life to the full. After much soul searching and lots of agonising I consciously stopped looking so far ahead, as I really was driving myself mad and I just couldn't cope anymore with thinking beyond the immediate future. Instead I started savouring each day as a gift and living it to the best of my ability as one day at a time was as much as I could handle. Do you know what, a strange thing happened; I started to notice things that I hadn't really noticed before. I started to enjoy the simplest of things and most importantly I learned the wonderful gift of acceptance, and with that, the realisation that today is all anybody has at any one time.

By making the conscious decision to really live each day and allow nature take it's course it intensified the present for me and so the future no longer seemed as important. Instead, it became more important to capture the essence of every moment. I learned to accept each of those moments as a gift and also to accept whatever the future would bring knowing there just aren't always answers. In this acceptance I stopped trying to control and by doing this, a lot of the worry that went with that control disappeared and things still worked out in their own time and way. I'm not saying that I have become a totally carefree human being as having that bone scan five years later proves. I still worry over the silliest of things, but I am able to see it for what it is. Especially when it is allowed to take control...just a useless habit and waste of time and energy.

The single most important thing I have learned from the whole cancer experience is the importance of living in the present moment. All our problems begin when we don't do this, one of them being that we allow worry to control us. We worry about the past, about the future but what most of us don't realise is, we rarely worry about the present moment. We drive ourselves mad over things we said or did in the past, when really the past is over and done with, it's no longer here so it cannot be changed. On the other hand, we anticipate and worry about future events that may or may not happen. As a result of being so busy doing this we are rarely anxious about the actual moment we are in at any one time. This is because we are so caught up with the past or the future or whatever the case maybe. We have all, at some stage, been sick with worry for weeks, even months before an anticipated event. The fear of all sorts of imagined scenarios even driving us mad. Yet, when the time eventually arrives, to our surprise, we often find ourselves totally relaxed and calm. The fear and anticipation of the event is often so much greater than the actual event it'self. So, you see, all that anxiety and fear can be a complete waste of time and energy.

I can identify with this scenario very easily. A few months before my diagnosis someone I knew had a mastectomy and subsequent chemotherapy. When I heard the news I remember thinking it would be my ultimate nightmare because cancer is a fear we all have. Sometimes we don't even realise this because we don't always confront our fears but they are there whether we choose to acknowledge them or not. Then, a few months later I was being confronted with that very same nightmare and it wasn't as bad as I had always anticipated it to be. Don't get me wrong, it was by no means plain sailing, but it wasn't as dreadful as I thought. The world didn't stop just because I was sick, and life still had to continue. Children had to be fed, work had to be done and the circle of life, no matter how difficult just kept on going. Think about what I have just said and ask yourself to stop for a moment and focus on what you are doing right now. Whether you are sick or well I'm sure you will discover that you are automatically doing whatever it is without giving it too much thought. Ask yourself then, if there are any worrying thoughts lurking in the recesses of your mind, what are they about. You'll probably discover they are usually about some event in the past or the future, definitely not the present moment. So you are missing out on an awful lot of not only 'present moments' but precious ones as well. The moral of the story is of course, if only we could all live in the here and now our lives would be just plain sailing...I make it sound so easy and simple don't I? But, of course, things are never that simple as life has a habit of often being rather complicated. We are human beings and it's our nature to try and control. We have fears about all sorts and rather than trying to confront them we bury them deeper. As humans we like to control and plan our lives but by doing this constantly we bring unnecessary worry upon ourselves. In our quest for control we end up worrying about all these planned happenings and events. When I was first diagnosed I was overwhelmed with tension and was being constantly told to relax and be positive. The thing was though I didn't know how to do all these things. I knew I was under pressure but I needed more that being told to cop on to myself. I had to learn how to do it.

What I now realise is we are all fearful beings whether we are sick or well, but a lot of the time we don't even know it. Often, unconsciously, we create our own fears. We fight against our own calm and so we stop ourselves from our basic right as individuals to be happy .By doing this we are creating our own sadness and yes even our own bad health. Remember now; I said we are unconsciously doing this; we don't set out to make ourselves sick or unhappy. If we realise this, we can then begin to make some changes to our way of thinking, by accepting that a lot of what we do is a habit and we all have the power to change habit's. We can then begin to improve our way of thinking because we come to see that we continuously create through thought without even realising it. We do attract what we fear so if we continue to worry about getting sick it will happen. Apart from the strain on our emotional and mental state, it causes all sorts of physical symptoms that are too numerous to mention. We only have to look at someone's outer physical appearance to see the deterioration it can bring to them. As this is allowed to continue the whole body becomes tense, stiff and unyielding so is it any wonder that sickness in some form is the outcome? On the other hand if we fear little we will attract good because what we subconsciously send out we do receive back. If we send out good thoughts we receive good back whereas if we send out toxic worrying thoughts we will attract negativity back. We get what we give and so constant complaining will attract complainers and on the other hand happy and positive thoughts will attract those with a similar disposition towards us.

It has to be said that friendships based on mutual misery is hard to sustain. We should also accept that we are all part of something that is so much bigger than who we are. If we realise that we are all individuals on our own journey. If we hand over and accept each day as the gift that it is. Our need to control and to plan would lessen, and in this letting go, so too would the worry that goes with it. We would then learn to accept what comes our way, and the way of those around us, in the realisation that the universe will continue to carve out it's own unique path for us.

But once again I have to say it's not that simple and one of the worst things that anyone can say to someone else is 'not to worry,' especially when there is something big going on in their lives. Even when all seems well we still find reasons to do it, even over the silliest of things. One person's worries may seem trivial to another. The person faced with a life threatening illness may scorn at the person who is fretting over something as seemingly mundane as getting to work on time; it's all relevant and everyone's own worries are unique to the individual. How big they seem depends on each person's frame of mind or where they are in their lives. When I was diagnosed with cancer the sense of fear was so great that I was intolerant of other people's seemingly pointless concerns in their lives. Those very insignificant concerns were once important to me before cancer took over so none of us have the right to tell another person to stop. We aren't walking in their shoes and we can't see inside their heads. Of course we worry, we wouldn't be human if we didn't. That worry can really get out of control when we are faced with something as life threatening as cancer. The list is endless... sickness, loss of control, hair loss, even death. Being told not to do it in this situation is denying us the right to experience and confront our very real emotions and so diminishes the whole experience. This makes us feel inadequate and weak for wanting to feel and express our fears, making us feel that we should bury them instead which of course only puts us under even more pressure. Trying to do this means a constant fight to keep busy, to avoid being alone with ourselves just in case those fears come to the surface. We may try to protect ourselves from the reality by detaching, by denying all that is happening. We may try to rescue and save others, help every-one else with their problems, anything rather than confront our own. All the time while we are doing this, what we fear continues to grow in strength. Increasing it's hold over us so we have to work even harder to keep in control. Eventually at some stage we just can't keep running and so something has to give. It just doesn't go away. It remains chronic, deplet-ing our energy and manifesting it'self in all sorts of erratic behaviour such as loss of sleep, anger, over activity etc. We can't escape our past, everything that happens to us remains with us until we are ready to deal with it.

Sometimes a seemingly insignificant hiccup maybe the thing that triggers all these hidden emotions. Fear of the un-known will continue this way. If, on the other hand, we try to face what we fear, become acquainted with it, look at it in the cold light of day, it does lessen it's hold over us. By doing this it loses some of it's power and we are taking back some control once again. When you are faced with a life threaten-ing illness one of the obvious fears is, of course, about the fact that you may die. Being told then 'you'll be fine' totally demeans that fear and denies you the right to express and confront that reality. In fact, I have to say, it has to be one of the most unrealistic statements one can make in that situation. I know from my experience the possibility of dying and facing my own mortality was one of the biggest things to ever happen to me. For a while I wasn't ready to face or confront these fears and I suppose in a way I was happy to play the game of being told I would be fine. Those fears were never too far away and kept popping into my consciousness when I least expected. As I tried to deny them they became more and more impossible to run from.

I remember being in a shop and picking up a book about breast cancer. In it they discussed various prognosis for different grades of cancers. It was the first time that I looked at this reality in bold print and I have to say I nearly fainted there and then as the sheer intensity of fear and panic hit me. For a while after I nearly drove myself mad. Being the inquisitive person I am I started reading all sorts of books about death and dying and do you know what, in my exploring I actually learned a hell of a lot about living. Getting acquainted with it gradually lessened it's hold over me. I planned my funeral, wrote numerous letters to my friends and family and having done all that I decided to put the whole thing away and get on with my life. Of course I want to live for a long time yet and I still have fears about death and dying but you see because I confront these fears, when they resurface, which they do again and again I don't feel the need to run and hide. By becoming acquainted with them they no longer hold as much power over me and I am not afraid of being afraid. Instead of trying to deny their presence, I allow the feelings to come to the surface. I accept them as part of who I am and give them time. By doing so the fear usually diminishes all on it's own until they resurface again which they will inevitably do, but never with the same intensity as that day in the book shop. Fear runs riot when we don't know what it is that we are afraid of, it takes us over and becomes like a poison that is out of our control.

When I got over the initial shock of cancer it gave me an opportunity to explore and re-evaluate my life. For a long time I was obsessed with time and how much of it I had. Gradually with the help of exploring various therapies like counselling, meditation, and many other things that I speak about in this book the focus shifted from the fear of recurrence to the fullness and intensity of the present. Through these various therapies I began changing the habit's of a lifetime of constantly planning ahead and anticipating all sorts of scenarios. I learned to slow down, relax, and so value and live in the here and now. By living in the present each day brings endless moments that I wouldn't normally otherwise have noticed. Things I would have worried about seem to work out all on their own. Instead of planning and making lists of things that "have" to be done I try to let things happen in a more natural way instead of trying to continuously control. It doesn't matter what stage you are at in your life. Whether you are healthy, newly diagnosed, terminally ill or facing any crisis in your life your worries will be uniquely yours. I can't emphasise it enough they must be acknowledged and so you must deal with them as realistically as you can and in whatever way you know how. Fear can be an education because once we explore it fully we realise just how weak we are. Once we face the centre of our fears only then do we become stronger as human beings. Sometimes, of course, a certain amount of fear has it's uses and serves to protect us on our journey through life. Our instinctive fear of someone or something should never be ignored as it may save us from a harmful situation. Our body's natural fight and flight mechanisms come into play as a response to our fear, which serves us well in the short term. If we live our lives permanently in this "fight or flight" state we really do run into all sorts of problems. We have all experienced this state when confronted with a sudden fright or shock, increased heart rate, rapid breathing, sweaty palms are just a few of the symptoms associated with it. While on one hand it has it's uses, imagine the long term effect these symptoms would have on our bodies if we are constantly in this state. We would literally make ourselves ill. The thing is to keep a sense of balance and control and not allow it to become a continuous influence in our lives.

We all know people who seem to sail through life without a care in the world! in fact they seem to have been born that way. On the other hand there are people who worry incessantly about everything to the point where there is no room for enjoyment in their lives. Whatever category we come under, we need to realise and accept ourselves, acknowledge it and then deal with it as best we can. We need to find ways to face and deal with our fears and so bring a sense of balance to our lives. Positive visualisation was one of the many tools I used to help me on my road to recovery. I believe it really did play a very big part in my getting well. The idea being that I trained my mind to focus and visualise on what I wanted or would like to happen in the future. At the time I was going through my chemotherapy this was a constant image of being healthy and cancer free. It really is a very powerful exercise and fills you with positive thoughts especially when you make it a part of your daily life. When we allow worry to take over we are doing the very opposite of this, i.e. we are creating images in our mind of what we fear may happen in the future. Of course we can't ignore either way of thinking but the thing to do is to give time to both emotions by balancing the negative image with the positive ones. As we do this, the positive images become more frequent and so the fear lessens and loses some of it's power over us. It's not always easy to confront our darkest fears and it can be even harder to express them to someone. If you are like me and this proves very difficult it's good to begin by writing these thoughts down on paper. No one needs to see it except yourself and it really is a very good place to start. You can happily scribble away to your heart's content safe in the knowledge that only you alone can see it. When you are finished you don't even have to read it. The important thing is you have expressed your thoughts rather than holding on to them. They are out of your consciousness and so the best thing is to dispose of them without ever reading over what you have written.

By writing them down you are beginning to deal with them and when you are ready and the time is right you can take things a step further and seek extra help through counselling. Often it is good to talk to someone who has no emotional attachment to you. Sometimes we don't want to overburden our loved ones with all of our fears and woes. Once you have made the first step by confronting these fears the path to healing does get easier.

Through our fears we come to realise that life is a combination of darkness and light, good and bad. If we accept this we also come to realise that the darkness does pass and the good prevails. No matter whether we are sick or well we are all vulnerable. Fear has the ability to show us just how vulnerable we really are and so it does take courage to confront that inner part of ourselves. No matter how tough anyone seems to be there is always that core of softness hidden somewhere even though we may choose to ignore it.

Our true and lasting healing begins when we acknowledge this and confront our fears. When we also acknowledge that no outer thing can really hurt us inside, we are only hurt by how we choose to look at and how we react to it. Unless we are mentally ill we have control over our attitude no matter how bad things seem to get. We have the gift of choice and so can choose how to deal with it. As I come to the end of this chapter I do hope it has given you some food for thought at whatever stage of your life you are at. We all deserve to be at peace in our lives even when we are faced with seemingly huge obstacles and tests of our endurance. Through these very tests and suffering we truly become stronger and richer from the experience. Of course, we would all love to sail through life without experiencing pain. A soul that is never touched by pain will never know the joy of coming through the dark times. Of really waking up to the sheer pleasure in the very simplest of things and the absolute joy of living no matter how flawed and imperfect they are.

I like the person I've become and have no desire to be a teenager again. I love being the age I am. There really are advantages to growing older and wiser and I feel I fast-forwarded a lot of learning time by getting cancer. I know I'm not going to live forever but while I'm still here I'm not going to waste time over what might have been and what maybe. I can say "no" and mean it and can say "yes" and mean it too. I still rant and rave about all sorts and drive my family mad at times. I still worry. I cry over all sorts of seemingly minor things but I experience moments of pure happiness and joy as well. I love being able to touch all of these emotions within me. The good and the bad, the darkness and the light. They are in us all and make us who we are, and I wouldn't want to have it any other way. I'm not afraid to say how I feel and by doing so I hope it helps others to realise that it's okay to be scared...to be sad. We don't have to be constantly smiling no matter how much pressure there seems to be on us to do so, what's most important is that we are true to ourselves at all times. Oh! and on a lovely final note my bone scan was clear. Isn't that good news...winning the lotto is good news but being told you are healthy and well is just the sweetest and best news ever. Before my cancer experience winning the lotto would have been high on my wish list, from where I'm sitting now it's not so important any more... how things change. It really does depend on where you are coming from...doesn't it?